Telling Your Story

Telling Your Story

A Step-by-Step Guide to Drafting Persuasive Legal Resumes and Cover Letters

Jo Ellen Dardick Lewis

Professor of Practice and Director of Legal Practice

Washington University in St. Louis School of Law

Carolina Academic Press

Durham, North Carolina

Library of Congress Cataloging-in-Publication Data

Names: Lewis, Jo Ellen Dardick, author.
Title: Telling your story : a step-by-step guide to drafting persuasive legal
  resumes and cover letters / Jo Ellen Dardick Lewis.
Description: Durham, North Carolina : Carolina Academic Press, LLC, 2017. |
  Includes bibliographical references and index.
Identifiers: LCCN 2016058569 | ISBN 9781611638899 (alk. paper)
Subjects: LCSH: Law--Vocational guidance--United States. | Job
  hunting--United States. | Cover letters--United States. | Résumés
  (Employment)--United States.
Classification: LCC KF297 .L49 2017 | DDC 650.14/2--dc23
LC record available at https://lccn.loc.gov/2016058569

Carolina Academic Press, LLC
700 Kent Street
Durham, North Carolina 27701
Telephone (919) 489-7486
Fax (919) 493-5668
www.cap-press.com

Printed in the United States of America

This book is dedicated to my students — past, present, and future. I appreciate you sharing your stories with me and look forward to hearing about your next chapters.

———————

To my husband, Roger, and our boys, Jake, Hal, and Seth — every day you inspire me. To my parents, Alec and Harriet Dardick, z"l, who always had confidence in me and made me believe that I could do anything.

JDL

Contents

Part II
Cover Letters

Part III
Writing Samples, References and
Recommendation Letters, and Networking

Appendices

Acknowledgments

There are many people who assisted me in the drafting and production of this book.

First, I am deeply grateful to my editor, Emily Shelton, and to Lydia Duran, marketing and communications design student at Washington University in St. Louis. Emily's careful eye and thoughtful comments helped me convey what I intended to. Lydia developed the templates for, and created all of, the samples throughout the book. Her creativity and work ethic are phenomenal. Thank you also to Grace Pledger, at Carolina Academic Press, who assisted us by finding a way to make the template we wanted to use actually work. My assistant, Jamie Roggen, was so helpful and always willing to make edits, again and again. Thank you, Jamie.

Second, thank you to my sister, Micki, for reading many versions of several chapters early on. Her insights and advice were so helpful to me.

Finally, thank you to my amazing colleagues, Ann, Jane, and Denise. Your teaching expertise and enthusiasm is contagious. Many of our conversations about how we can assist our students in reaching their professional goals are in this book in one form or another.

JDL

Message to Students — Why Did I Write This Book?

> You have brains in your head.
> You have feet in your shoes.
> You can steer yourself
> Any direction you choose.
> *Oh, the Places You'll Go!*
> Dr. Seuss[1]

Everyone has a story, and in a professional context, you will tell your own in a resume and cover letter. Your resume and cover letter are two of the most important pieces of persuasive writing that you will ever draft. Putting together a memorable resume which reflects your individuality and strengths takes time, but is well worth the effort. You are your own best advocate, and writing your resume and cover letter is your first opportunity to sell yourself. A strong resume persuades a prospective legal organization — let's call this an "Employer" — that you are someone whom that Employer should consider hiring.

I have worked with law students for over twenty years, helping them draft the persuasive resumes and cover letters that get them interviews and jobs. Most of this work happens in a crisis mode: before a career services resume drop deadline, after meeting a prospective Employer at a networking event, or right before winter break. This book teaches you how to avoid the crisis mode by drafting your resume and cover letter the way you learned legal writing: one step at a time. If you spend fifteen to thirty minutes each week drafting your resume and cover letter, they will be finished by the end of the semester.

As you will learn in law school, all writing has an *audience* and serves a *purpose*. The *audience* for your resume will be someone connected with, or someone who can connect you with, an Employer. That person may or may not know anything about you, the law school you attend, or the high caliber of its students. This means that you are writing your resume for several audiences. Those audiences could be: 1) an attorney with an Employer; 2) a human resources professional; 3) a friend or relative; or 4) a professor or law school career development advisor from whom you are seeking advice. The more information you can provide about yourself and your accomplishments and strengths, the more that audience can assist you in connecting with an appropriate Employer.

---

1. Dr. Seuss, *Oh, the Places You'll Go!* (Random House, Inc., 1990), p. 2.

I want to emphasize just how important it is to be open to tailoring your resume, when meeting with any of your audiences, in order to take advantage of their feedback — especially the career development office at your law school. Your career advisor is the eyes and ears of your law school in terms of prospective employment, and has the resources to know where other students have been successful and how to use those students' successes as a model for you.

After determining your *audience*, you want to identify the *purpose* of your resume. The purpose of your resume is to get an Employer so interested in your story that the Employer must speak to you — thus, the interview and, ultimately, the job offer.

So, if right now you are thinking that this is one of those ten or twelve step books, you are close. I don't know if there are exactly ten or twelve steps, but I do know that if you draft your resume one step at a time, the task will not be overwhelming and it will get done. I will warn you that when you make the transition from a general resume to a legal resume, the first draft is the most difficult, as it will require you to look at yourself through the eyes of an Employer. But bear in mind that all law students have skills and accomplishments that are directly applicable to legal employment, and possess the characteristics that make for effective lawyers. Those accomplishments, skills, and characteristics form the basis of your story. Your resume and cover letter are the vehicles for telling that story. And as your personal story evolves, your resume will evolve as well.

Let's get started telling your story!

Professor Jo Ellen Dardick Lewis

Telling Your Story

Chapter 1

Introduction: How Can I Use This Book to Help Me Get a Job?

The goal of this book is to assist you in obtaining a job after your 1L, 2L, or 3L year. As you know, to obtain that job, you must have a persuasive resume. Your resume should be so compelling that it convinces an Employer that you would be an asset to their organization.

Truthfulness

In drafting your resume and cover letter, the first and most important thing is to be one hundred percent truthful. There is no quicker way to lose your credibility with an Employer than by including false information on your resume. Unfortunately, I have known students who have lost jobs and suffered consequences in their law school careers and beyond because they falsified information. You'll want to start your legal career with the same high ethical standards that you will maintain throughout your practice.

Organization of Book

Each chapter of this book is organized around one section of your resume or cover letter. First, you will learn about the purpose of that section. Second, you will read detailed instructions about how to draft it. Third, you will find additional tips for international students who are studying in American law schools and are interested in working with American law firms either in the U.S. or overseas. Fourth, you will see examples of resumes and cover letters drafted by students just like you, both before and after they applied the principles outlined in this book. (Please note that because the *before* resumes and cover letters are by real students, some of them contain spelling, grammatical, and other errors. As you would expect, those errors are corrected in the students' *after* resumes and cover letters.) Finally, at the end of each chapter there is a checklist for you to see whether or not you incorporated the book's suggestions. (A word of caution about checklists: they are only worthwhile if you actually "check off" each item. Often when I meet with a student and see a checklist with all of the items checked off and then ask the student to show me a particular item, he or she is not able to do so. Chances are that the student mentally "checked off" each item but did not physically do so on the document itself.)

Student Questionnaire

To help you in drafting your resume with prospective Employers in mind, please answer the questions in the Student Questionnaire in Appendix A. If you do not know the answers to some of the questions at this time, don't worry; just answer, "I don't know." Law school — especially your 1L and 2L years and the summers following those years — is a time of exploration, and you may not have specific career goals yet. When you meet with a professor or career advisor, be sure to bring your completed questionnaire to the meeting; it will help them to understand and assist you better.

Students' Sample Resumes and Cover Letters

If you are curious to know more about the students who worked with me and contributed "before and after" resumes and cover letters to this book, you'll find their stories in Appendix B. The students' final, completed resumes are included in Appendix C and several final cover letters in Appendix D. (For the purposes of this book, students' identifying information has been altered to protect their privacy.) I am convinced that the steps in this book will work for you as they have for my students. All of them secured incredible legal internships after their 1L year. Read the Epilogue to learn where they interned.

Typeface and Font for Resumes and Cover Letters

Since the purpose of your resume and cover letter is to make it easy for your audience to see your accomplishments, you'll want to use a typeface that makes the actual words easy to read. Legal writers and readers are fairly conservative and accustomed to seeing legal writing in certain fonts; since your goal is to become one of those legal writers and readers, use one that they expect to see. What is actually *on* your resume will make you stand out from the other applicants, not the typeface you choose. By far the most common typeface for a resume and cover letter in hard copy is Times New Roman, black, in 9- to 12-point font. Another serif font (with tails), such as Courier New, is also typical. If your resume and cover letter are sent electronically, consider using a sans serif font (no tails), like Arial or Tahoma. Documents look different on a computer screen vs. on paper, so keep that in mind when picking a font.

One last word about font: regardless of which you choose, you'll want to use it consistently in your resume and cover letter. You can, however, vary the size to emphasize certain words. For example, using a slightly larger size for your name on your resume will make it stand out; bold, underline, or italics for the name of each section of your resume, your former employer, or your job title will highlight those sections or words.

Before you get started on your resume, let's take a look at a few complete *before* and *after* resumes. They were written by law students like you who have many accomplishments and strengths to share with Employers, but who needed to take the resumes they used to apply to law school and transform them into legal resumes. Review each *before* and *after* resume as if you are an Employer and ask yourself: Whom do you want to meet and invite to interview for a legal job — the person represented by the *before* resume or the *after* resume? Notice what a difference an effective resume can make in telling that same person's story.

Chapter 1

Sample Resumes

Examples of Complete Resumes — Before and After

Before

Sample resume of Laura Mackey (0–1 year experience).

Laura Mary Mackey
1234 Canyon Ridge Dr. #109 Riverside, CA 92507
laura.m.mackey@gmail.com
805.123.4567

Education

University of California, Riverside	**2013-Present**

Major: Political Science, Law and Society
GPA: X.XX

Santa Barbara City College	**2008- 2013**

Associates Degree: Political Science, Liberal Arts
Major: Political Science
GPA: X.XX

Boston University	**2007-2008**

Major: Biology

Work Experience

United States Pretrial Services	**January 2014-June 2014**

Intern
- Assisted Officers during court proceedings
- Observed Pretrial interviews and report processes

Santa Barbara Superior Court	**October 2011-August 2013**

Own Recognizance Investigator
- Began as an intern/volunteer and was promoted to paid Judicial Assistant II
- Interview inmates and prepare reports for the Judges to determine the defendant's custody status
- Work as a liaison between the Court and local arresting agencies
- Help inmates and their friends/family understand and navigate the legal process

Santa Barbara City College Internship	**April 2013**

Political Science Department
- Observed and interacted with numerous lawmakers in Sacramento to gain a deeper understanding of state-level politics

Jackson Medical Group	**October 2008- June 2012**

Billing Assistant
- Submitted patients' visits to insurance companies.
- Helped disgruntled patients frustrated with the medical billing process
- Deposited and balanced insurance payments

Achievements

President's Honor List	**2012**

Santa Barbara City College

Chancellor's Honor List	**2013-2014**

University of California, Riverside

Dean's Academic Distinction Award	**2014**

University of California, Riverside

Pi Sigma Alpha Member	**Spring 2014-Present**

Political Science Honors Society
University of California, Riverside

Extracurricular Involvement

Mock Trial	**2013-Present**

University of California, Riverside
- Vice President

Foreign Language
Spanish
- Reading, Comprehension and Writing: Advanced
- Speaking: Intermediate

After

Edited sample resume of Laura Mackey (0–1 year experience).

Laura Mary Mackey

123 Westgate Ave #6   805.123.4567
St. Louis, MO 63130   lmm@wustl.edu

Education

Washington University School of Law   **St. Louis, MO**
J.D. Candidate   May 2018
   Honors and Activities
      Recipient: Scholar of Law Scholarship (merit-based, $X/year for 3 years)
      Member: Women's Law Caucus; American Constitution Society
      Participant: Client Counseling Competition

University of California, Riverside   **Riverside, CA**
B.A., Political Science, Law and Society, *summa cum laude*   June 2015
   Honors and Activities
      Recipient: Dean's Honor List (3 consecutive quarters with GPA of at least X.X) and Dean's Academic
        Distinction Award (required GPA of at least X.X)
      Vice President (elected position, 2014-2015); member (2013-2015) - Mock Trial
        As Vice President team won Honorable Mention at local competition (1st time for UCR). Worked with team
        members to improve direct and cross-examination questions and techniques. Organized and ran practices.

Santa Barbara City College   **Santa Barbara, CA**
A.A., Political Science   May 2013
      Recipient: President's Honor List (required GPA of at least X.X)

Boston University   **Boston, MA**
                                                                        May 2008

Legally Related Experience

United States Pretrial Services   **Riverside, CA**
Intern   January 2014-June 2014
      Observed U.S. Pretrial Officers during initial bail hearings, bail reviews, and inmate interviews. Verified
      criminal records. Coordinated inmate intake with federal agencies including FBI, DEA, U.S. Marshals.

Santa Barbara Superior Court   **Santa Barbara, CA**
Own Recognizance Investigator   October 2011-August 2013
      Began as an intern and promoted to paid Judicial Assistant II within four months. Interviewed inmates at county
      jail and drafted custody status reports for judges. Reviewed inmates' prior criminal records. Reviewed Probable
      Cause Declarations and submitted to judges. Completed bail increase/reduction documents and release
      paperwork and submitted documents to custody officers. Researched Los Angeles County bail schedule. Served
      as liaison between Court and sheriff's department, police department, probation officers, and parole officers.
      Assisted inmates and their friends/family in understanding and navigating the legal process.

Other Professional Experience

Jackson Medical Group   **Santa Barbara, CA**
(General Practice Group with 12 physicians in 4 offices)
Billing Assistant   October 2008-June 2012
      Submitted records of patients' visits to insurance companies. Deposited and balanced insurance payments.
      Worked with major national insurance companies such as Blue Cross, Blue Shield, Cigna, and AARP as well as
      Medicare. All tasks complied with HIPAA regulations. Assisted patients in resolving conflicts with insurance
      companies.

Interests
      Ran two marathons. Hiked Mt. Whitney (14,509 ft., highest mountain in contiguous United States).

Foreign Language
   Spanish
      Speaking: Limited Working Proficiency. Reading: Limited Working Proficiency.

Before

Sample resume of Matthew Novack (2–3 years experience).

Matthew T. Novack

matthew@gmail.com
(845) 123-4567

1414 Commonwealth Ave. #28
Boston, Massachusetts 02134

EDUCATION
Boston University Class of 2013
- Bachelor of Arts in Psychology; Certificate in Criminal Justice.
- Dean's List.
- Sigma Alpha Lambda Honor Society.

Don Bosco Preparatory High School Class of 2009

PROFESSIONAL EXPERIENCE
Office of Dr. Frederick Winsmann, PhD., Clinical and Forensic Psychologist
Forensic Psychology Research Assistant (March 2014 – Present)
- Research and analyze criminal and civil patterns of behavior for use in certified reports, which help to determine criminal responsibility, risk of reoffending, competency to stand trial and mental health civil commitment in felony criminal cases.
- Condense thousands of pages of legal and medical records for use in reports to be referenced by attorneys, judges and mental health professionals.
- Analyze legal documents, and research statutes and case law pertaining to mental health commitment and competency to stand trial.
- Adhere to strict industry standards of quality and confidentiality.

Avention, Inc. (Formerly OneSource Information Services)
Market Research Analyst (March 2014 – Present)
- Gather and analyze competitive intelligence information including corporate strategy and risk, research and development expenditures, emerging markets, strategic initiatives, corporate restructuring, enterprise information technology infrastructure composition and requirements, intra-company production and development methodologies (Six-Sigma, Agile, Waterfall, Scrum).
- Manage database information and use enterprise content management system to publish quarterly custom market research reports on more than 100 Fortune 1000 companies in dozens of industries.
- Analyze SEC filings, annual reports, quarterly reports, corporate finances and earnings calls.
- Track corporate capital expenditures, with an emphasis on IT software and hardware expenditures.
- Research financial and information technology trends on enterprise- and industry-wide scale.
- Maintain, purge and regularly update relational databases containing several million data points.
- Collaborated with QA team to perform quality assurance testing of custom news aggregator product.

Advocates, Inc.
Direct Care Counselor / Health Record Coordinator (May 2013 – December 2013)
- Helped patients navigate legal and mental health systems.
- Designed and implemented mental health treatment plans.
- Advised patients on methods of achieving financial and social independence.
- Evaluated patients for psychological symptoms and effectiveness of prescribed medication.
- Managed patient health record and rehabilitation database.

Rockland County, New York Courthouse
Judicial Intern to The Honorable Judge William Nelson (Summer 2012)
- Shadowed Judge Nelson through criminal trials and hearings, and in meetings with assistant district attorneys and criminal defense attorneys.
- Performed legal research and advised the judge on relevant matters of case law pertaining to current cases.
- Analyzed courtroom proceedings with Judge Nelson, his principal law clerk, attorneys and other interns.
- Proofread legal motions and briefs.
- Facilitated communication between the Judge Nelson and other judges, clerks and attorneys.

After

Edited sample resume of Matthew Novack (2–3 years experience).

Matthew T. Novack
(845) 123-4567 mtnovack@wustl.edu

Permanent Address: School Address:
16 Adams Court, Nanuet, NY 10954   7025 Forsyth Dr., St. Louis, MO 63105

EDUCATION
Washington University School of Law, JD Candidate   *May 2018*
Honors and Activities
- Recipient: Scholar in Law (merit-based XX% tuition scholarship for three years)
- Recipient: William R. and Nancy J. Hirsch Scholarship (merit-based XX% tuition scholarship for three years)
- 1L Elected Representative: IP Law Society
- 1L Appointed Representative: Employment Law Society
- Participant: Client Counseling & Interviewing Competition
- Member: Negotiation and Dispute Resolution Society

Boston University, B.A., Psychology   *May 2013*
Honors and Activities
- Dean's List
- Member: Kappa Sigma Fraternity
- Member: Sigma Alpha Lambda Honor Society

LAW-RELATED EXPERIENCE
Office of Frederick Winsmann, PhD, Clinical and Forensic Psychologist, Boston, Massachusetts.
Forensic Psychology Research Assistant   *March 2014 – Present*
Research and analyze criminal and behavioral patterns using legal, medical, and personal records for use in forensic reports to help evaluate criminal responsibility, risk of reoffending, competency to stand trial, and SVP civil commitment. Draft sections of forensic reports for submission to federal and state courts. Review and incorporate legal documents and research statutes pertaining to mental health commitment and competency to stand trial. Adhere to strict industry standards of quality and confidentiality. File trademark application with USPTO for continuing education symposium on psychology and the law.

Rockland County District Court, New City, New York.
Judicial Intern   *Summer 2012*
Observed criminal trials and hearings, and meetings between assistant district attorneys, defense attorneys, and judges. Performed basic legal research and discussed relevant matters of case law pertaining to current cases with judge. Relayed information between judges, clerks, and attorneys.

BUSINESS EXPERIENCE
Avention, Inc. (Formerly OneSource Information Services – 200+ employees), Concord, Massachusetts.
Market Research Analyst   *March 2014–August 2015*
Researched and analyzed competitive intelligence information including corporate strategy and risk, research and development expenditures, emerging markets, strategic initiatives, corporate restructuring, enterprise information technology infrastructure composition and requirements, intra-company production and development methodologies (Six-Sigma, Agile, Waterfall, Scrum). Analyzed SEC filings, annual reports, quarterly reports, corporate finances and earnings calls. Researched financial and information technology trends on enterprise- and industry-wide scale. Tracked corporate capital expenditures with an emphasis on IT software and hardware expenditures. Maintained, purged, and regularly updated database information. Used enterprise content management system to publish quarterly custom market research reports on more than 100 Fortune 1000 companies in dozens of industries.

OTHER PROFESSIONAL EXPERIENCE
Advocates, Inc., Dedham, Massachusetts.

Direct Care Counselor   *May 2013–December 2013*
Assisted in the design and implementation of individualized mental health treatment plans. Helped evaluate patients for psychological symptoms and effectiveness of prescribed medication.

INTERESTS: Boating, swimming, wakeboarding, waterskiing, snowboarding, and playing guitar.

Before

Sample resume of Stacy Stevens (more than 3 years experience).

123 SMITHTON ST. • LAPLACE, LA 70068
STACYSTEVENS@YAHOO.COM • 123-4567 (CELL)
STACY STEVENS

EDUCATION & HONORS

Rice University, Houston, TX   August 2007-May 2011
Bachelor of Arts in Sociology awarded on: May 14, 2011 (GPA: X.XX/4.00)
- **Magna Cum Laude**
- **Phi Beta Kappa**
- President's Honor Roll: *Maintained a GPA that was in the top 30% of undergraduates*
- Leadership Rice Summer Mentorship Experience Fellow
- Pre-Law Undergraduate Scholars (PLUS) Outstanding Student at UNL-Law Program

University of Paris IV- Sorbonne, Paris, France   Spring 2010
Completed a study abroad program that focused on French language, history, and culture

EXPERIENCE

The World Race   **Asia, Europe, Africa**
Logistics Coordinator   September 2013-August 2014
- Traveled to 11 countries in the span of 11 months as part of a missionary team
- Partnered with local organizations and ministries to serve the community and address social issues
- Led efforts to teach English, clean dumpsites, host children's camps, restore buildings, and distribute food
- Coordinated transportation, lodging, and administration for 40+ people

Jackson Elementary School   **Jackson, LA**
*Second Grade Teacher with **Teach for America***   July 2011-July 2013
- Developed over 20 lessons and activities per week, created resources, presented content on various topics
- Facilitated student growth of over 1.8 years in reading
- Managed 17 students in behavior and character development and addressed special needs a on case-by-case basis

Rice University Faculty Club   **Houston, TX**
Banquet Server/Waitress   January 2008-May 2011
- Facilitated satisfaction of over 150 customers through fulfillment of orders and resolution of complaints
- Improved atmosphere of facilities and maintained order of resources and supplies

The Impact Movement   **Orlando, FL**
Assistant to Director of Communications   Summer 2010
- Published a promotional article in two newspapers and forged a partnership between two organizations
- Redesigned marketing strategies and produced conference material for over 1500 attendees

U. S. Equal Employment Opportunity Commission   **Houston, TX**
Legal Intern/Mentee   Summer 2009
- Designed a large applicant database of over 300 contacts and located possible witnesses
- Conducted research on case facts and witness history and analyzed legal writings for accuracy
- Shadowed the lead attorney for his leadership abilities and completed leadership profiles of managers

ACTIVITIES

- Impact Movement, Conference Planner (2011-2012)
- Impact Movement, President (2007-2011)
- Black Student Union, Service Chair (2007-2011)
- Professional Development Advisor (2009-2011)
- Advocating Diversity Association (2008-2011)
- Melodious Voices Gospel Choir (2007-2011)
- Jones College Powderpuff Team (2007-2011)
- Leadership Rice Mentorship Experience (Summer 2009)
- Pre-Law Undergraduate Scholars (Summer 2008)

CERTIFICATIONS & SKILLS

- Certified teacher in Louisiana for grades 1-5 (2012-2015)
- Speak Intermediate French, write basic French, and speak basic Spanish

After

Edited sample resume of Stacy Stevens (more than 3 years experience).

7345 Yale Ave. Apt 2E   stacyastevens@wustl.edu
St. Louis, MO 63130   504-123-4567

Stacy A. Stevens

EDUCATION

Washington University School of Law   St. Louis, Missouri
J.D. Candidate   May 2018
Honors and Activities
- Recipient - Dean's Fellowship ($X tuition for three years, faculty mentor, research assistantship)
- Finalist - 1L Client Counseling Competition (one of 24 teams out of 72 participating)
- Member - Women's Law Caucus - Auction Committee Member (largest student-led fundraiser designated for 2L public interest summer stipend)
- Member - Public Service Advisory Board-Public Service Committee; Black Law Students Association; International Law Society

Rice University   Houston, Texas
Bachelor of Arts in Sociology, magna cum laude (GPA: X.XX/4.00)   May 2011
Honors and Activities
- Inductee - *Phi Beta Kappa*
- Recipient - QuestBridge Scholarship ($X tuition and living expenses for four years)
- President - The Impact Movement (Rice chapter of national org.) - collaborated with Asst. Dean for Students to plan initiatives, drafted proposals for organization funding, served as liaison between campus and national organization, spearheaded on-campus outreach, and coordinated logistics for national conference
- Community Service Chair - Black Students Association (elected position) - coordinated community events
- Member - Advocating Diversity Association - Event Committee Member - secured sponsorship from local businesses, obtained funding from student government, and allocated facilities for program use

PUBLIC SERVICE & NON-PROFIT EXPERIENCE

The World Race   Asia, Europe, Africa
Participant and Logistics Coordinator (appointed position)   September 2013-August 2014
Traveled to 11 countries in 11 months as part of missionary team; raised $15,500 in funds through presentations and letters to board members and individual investors; partnered with local organizations and ministries to combat human trafficking, teach English, feed and clothe orphans, clean townships, and restore buildings; coordinated transportation, lodging, and administration for 40+ people; and served as liaison between on-site team and headquarters' logistics leader.

The Impact Movement   Orlando, FL
Assistant to Director of Communications   Summer 2010
Drafted promotional article for *The Orlando Times* to publicize organization; coordinated regular publishing opportunities for organization; redesigned marketing strategies; and developed conference materials for 1500 attendees.

LEGALLY RELATED EXPERIENCE

U. S. Equal Employment Opportunity Commission   Houston, TX
Legal Intern/Mentee   Summer 2009
Conducted research on case facts and witness history; reviewed legal memos and briefs for accuracy; attended witness deposition; shadowed director of district office; designed applicant database of over 300 contacts; and located witnesses.

TEACHING EXPERIENCE

Teach for America - Jackson Elementary School   Jackson, LA
Second Grade Teacher   July 2011-July 2013
Developed over 20 lessons and activities per week; facilitated student growth of 1.8 years in reading; managed 17 students in behavior and character development; created specialized plan for student needs; forged critical parent and student relationships in furtherance of common goal; and campaigned for county-wide tax initiative to benefit students.

St. Charles Parish Schools   Destrehan, LA
Substitute Teacher   August 2014-May 2015
Assisted special education students in schoolwork and recreation activities; completed individualized student plans and tracking charts; and coordinated with parents to implement student-specific goals.

SKILLS & INTERESTS

Languages: French (Limited Working Proficiency) and Spanish (Elementary Proficiency)
Alto - Gospel Choir

Part I

Legal Resumes

Chapter 2

Identifying Information: Who Are You and How Can I Contact You?

Purpose of Section

The first section of your resume is where an Employer learns about you and how to contact you. Identifying information includes your name, address, phone number, and email. Let's take them one at a time.

Step-by-Step Guide

Name

Your legal resume creates an opportunity for you to identify the professional name you will use in your career. Law students often choose to use their legal names and not their nicknames for a legal resume; for example, a student whose legal name is Jacob but whose friends call him Jake will use Jacob professionally. Using your legal name on your resume is a good idea, as you will frequently need to show proof of identity before getting hired, typically with an official government-issued document. After you are hired, you can let your colleagues know if you prefer to be called by another name. Sometimes students put their nickname in parentheses next to their legal name, but this is unnecessary and can lead to confusion.

The only time it may be helpful to provide a legal name *and* a nickname is if you are an international student who has an "American" name in addition to a given one. Sometimes an American name can be easier for an Employer to pronounce and, even more importantly, it shows a connection to the U.S., especially if you are considering working there. (You'll find additional tips for international students at the end of the chapter.) As part of their professional names, attorneys also tend to use their middle initials on legal resumes and for signatures. I am not sure why, but given the large number of attorneys who do this, you will look like you belong to the profession if you do the same.

Address

Many law students underestimate how much the address they use on their resume can assist them in getting a job. While it is rare that an Employer will actually mail you a letter, your address serves a very useful purpose: it becomes a persuasive piece of your resume, because it indicates a connection to the city in which you plan to build your career. Given that you are a law student residing in the city of your law school, you should always include your law school address. If you want to practice in that city, then this is the only address you will include. If, however, you are interested in pursuing employment in a city other than the one in which your law school is located—i.e., a target city—you may want to include an additional address. For example, if you want to practice in Los Angeles and have family in that city, you would include the Los Angeles address as well as the school address, and call the Los Angeles address your "Home Address" or "Permanent Address." Be careful, though, not to put a target city address on your resume if it simply belongs to a friend. I understand that you want to show a connection, but it needs to be a real connection. (There are other ways to make one that we will see in later chapters.) If you do decide to include an address other than that of your law school city, make sure its residents know that you are using it.

Finally, some students wonder why they should put on their law school address at all if they don't want to practice in that city. The short answer is that you must be living somewhere, and an Employer is going to assume that you are living in the city in which you are attending law school. If that address is missing, an Employer might wonder if you are actually a current student.

Phone Number

Employers often call students to schedule interviews, so the phone number on your resume should be one that you do in fact answer. For most students, this means a cell phone number. If you happen to have a cell phone number that has an area code in your target city, this is another way for you to show your connection to it. This is not to suggest, however, that you should *get* a phone number with your target city's area code. Employers know that you have probably had your cell phone number for some time, and do not look askance if your area code is based in a city other than the one in which an Employer is located.

In addition to making sure that you answer the phone and check messages, make sure that your voicemail is working and that your outgoing message sounds professional. Speak in your own voice (don't use a recording) without any music or other background noise, and be sure to use the name on your resume. A typical outgoing message could be something like:

> "Hello, this is Jacob Smith and I am not able to answer your call at this time. Your call is very important to me, so please leave your name and a number where I can reach you and I will call you back as soon as possible. Thank you."

Email

Most Employers will contact you via email, so use your professional email, not a personal account. When you are a law student, your professional email is your law school email address. Students often have Gmail as their main email and want to use that on their resume, but this is problematic for a number of reasons. First, using your law school email address is another way of showing an Employer that you are in fact enrolled in that school. Second, if your Gmail account is your personal account, you likely receive a lot of mail there and might inadvertently skip over or forget to answer an Employer's message. Finally, many students have all of their law school emails "pushed" to their Gmail so that they only have to check one account. Big mistake. I have had several students tell me with regret that they missed important emails from potential Employers and thus deadlines for responding to job offers. In addition, university technology professionals have told me that the sophisticated filters in university systems frequently block or push certain emails to spam rather than to other systems, like Gmail. Keep it simple: use your law school email address, check it on at least a daily basis, and you will avoid the possibility of missing an important email.

One way to convey professionalism in your emails is to use an automatic signature block. Include your name, law school, degree and date of graduation, cell number, your LinkedIn link (see Chapter 14), and, if possible, the logo of your law school, and set this up as an automatically generated signature on all outgoing email.

One last point on identifying information: it also makes a great header for your cover letters. (You will learn more about this in later chapters.)

Additional Tips for International Students

Name

Employers want to pronounce your name correctly when speaking to you. To assist them, include your American name, if you have one, in addition to your given name. If your gender is not clear from your name and you want an Employer to know your gender, include an honorific - "Mr.," "Ms.," or "Mx." — before your name. In lieu of including a gender-identifying honorific on your resume, use an honorific in your signature block on your emails and cover letter.

Address

If you are seeking employment in a county other than in the U.S., include an address in that target country or city. As always, make sure that someone residing at that address knows you included it on your resume.

Phone Number

Use your American phone number and not your international phone number unless you are applying to an Employer located outside of the U.S. In the latter case, include both phone numbers.

Chapter 2

Sample Resumes

Identifying Information

Sample 2.1

Before

Resume of Frank Douglas (0–1 year experience).

Notes:

1. This is Frank's legal name, but he does not include his middle initial.

2. No law school address is listed. That needs to be added.

3. Including his cell phone is fine.

4. Frank needs to use his law school email and not his undergraduate email.

---

❶ Frank Douglas ❸
❷ 18 Chase Ct., Lawrenceville, NJ 08648 • (609) 123-4567 • fd@columbia.edu **❹**

EDUCATION

The Lawrenceville School, Lawrenceville, NJ   September 2006 - June 2010
High School Diploma

Columbia University, New York, NY   September 2010 - May 2014
Bachelor of Arts - Economics-Philosophy
Coursework:
    <u>Economics</u>
    Globalization and its Risks
    Economic Organization and Development of China
    International Trade
    Urban Economics
    <u>Philosophy</u>
    Philosophical Problems of Climate Change
    Philosophy of Law
    Ethics
    <u>Other/Interdisciplinary</u>
    Economics-Philosophy Seminar (Seminar focusing on the economic, philosophic, and
    political issues surrounding climate change)
    Introduction to Film Theory
    The Social World
    The Rise of Civilization
    Introduction to Comparative Politics

WORK EXPERIENCE

American School in Japan, Tokyo, Japan   July 2009-August 2009
Camp Counselor

Columbia University, New York, NY   June 2011-August 2011
General Assistant   June 2012-August 2012
-Performed basic assistant work in IT Department of Butler Library

Institute for Advanced Study, Princeton, NJ   June 2013-August 2013
Public Affairs Intern   June 2014-August 2014
-Duties consisted mostly of fact-checking and copy editor

EXTRACURRICULAR ACTIVITIES AND INTERESTS
Completed Leadership Training Course at YMCA Camp Mason, NJ, in July and August of 2008
Staff Writer for high school newspaper
Member of Young Democrats in high school
Member of Columbia Democrats in college
Special Interests in Cinema, American literature, and Japanese culture and language

LANGUAGES
Native speaker of English
Fluent in Italian and French
Reading knowledge of Spanish
Learning Japanese

Sample 2.2

After

Edited resume of Frank Douglas (0–1 year experience).

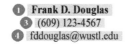

School Address:
1234 Lindell Blvd., Apt. W-504
St. Louis, MO 63108

Frank D. Douglas
(609) 123-4567
fddouglas@wustl.edu

Permanent Address:
18 Chase Ct.
Lawrenceville, NJ 08648

EDUCATION

Washington University School of Law   St. Louis, MO – 2018
J.D. Candidate
- Recipient - Scholar in Law Award ($X/year merit scholarship)
- Board Member - Energy and Environmental Law Society
- Member - International Law Society

Columbia University   New York, NY – 2014
B.A., Economics and Philosophy
- Dean's List - Fall 2013 & Spring 2014
- Op-Ed Writer - Columbia Spectator (school newspaper)
- Member - Columbia Democrats

PROFESSIONAL EXPERIENCE

Lutheran Social Ministries of New Jersey   Trenton, NJ – 2015
ESL Teacher
Taught adult classes in English. Worked with groups of varying ability to improve their grammar and vocabulary. Assisted in developing lessons and evaluating student ability through written and verbal tests. Taught citizenship classes to students attempting to gain U.S. citizenship, with lessons in history and civics.

Institute for Advanced Study   Princeton, NJ – 2013-2014
Public Affairs Intern
Reviewed and edited press releases. Updated website page on faculty publications and ran Excel functions to find anomalies in database cataloging term lengths of over 300 scholars. Collected biographical and autobiographical material on multiple faculty members. Drafted summaries of faculty members' life and work in preparation for retirement celebrations. Reviewed lists of scholars arriving from other institutions to make sure international institution names had been translated correctly.

Columbia University   New York, NY – 2011-2012
Information Technology General Assistant
Assisted IT department in hardware repairs and software installations on staff computers. Contacted Dell and Hewlett-Packard for information on warranties and to order replacements for malfunctioning material still covered under warranty.

American School in Japan   Tokyo, Japan – 2009
Camp Counselor
Responsible for group of 15 children aged 10-13. Assisted them in activities designed to aid them in learning English. Met with parents to discuss progress of children.

SPECIAL INTERESTS
American literature (Hemingway especially) and film (Film Noir, French New Wave)
Fan of football and soccer (played both in high school)
Member of Alumni Association of the Lawrenceville School, in NJ

LANGUAGES
Fluent in Italian and French
Reading knowledge of Spanish

Notes:

1. Frank added his middle initial to his full name, like attorneys do.

2. In addition to including a school address, Frank added his permanent address to show a connection to New Jersey, his target area.

3. Frank has changed his voicemail to sound professional. He checks it for messages at least twice per day.

4. He is using his official law school email and regularly checks it for emails from Employers.

Sample 2.3

Before

Resume of Matthew Novack (2–3 years experience).

Notes:

1. Matthew is using his full legal name, including his middle initial, so no changes are needed here.

2. Matthew needs to change his address to his law school address and perhaps include a permanent address if his target city is different than his law school city.

3. His cell phone number is fine, but Matthew will want to check his voicemail message to make sure it sounds professional.

4. As tempting as it is to use a Gmail account on your resume, using your law school email is more professional.

5. The outside border is distracting and should be deleted. It also uses up valuable space for important substantive information.

---

① Matthew T. Novack

matthew@gmail.com **④**
(845) 123-4567 **③**

② 1414 Commonwealth Ave. #28
Boston, Massachusetts 02134

EDUCATION   **⑤**
Boston University Class of 2013
- Bachelor of Arts in Psychology; Certificate in Criminal Justice.
- Dean's List.
- Sigma Alpha Lambda Honor Society.

Don Bosco Preparatory High School Class of 2009

PROFESSIONAL EXPERIENCE
Office of Dr. Frederick Winsmann, PhD., Clinical and Forensic Psychologist
Forensic Psychology Research Assistant (March 2014 – Present)
- Research and analyze criminal and civil patterns of behavior for use in certified reports, which help to determine criminal responsibility, risk of reoffending, competency to stand trial and mental health civil commitment in felony criminal cases.
- Condense thousands of pages of legal and medical records for use in reports to be referenced by attorneys, judges and mental health professionals.
- Analyze legal documents, and research statutes and case law pertaining to mental health commitment and competency to stand trial.
- Adhere to strict industry standards of quality and confidentiality.

Avention, Inc. (Formerly OneSource Information Services)
Market Research Analyst (March 2014 – Present)
- Gather and analyze competitive intelligence information including corporate strategy and risk, research and development expenditures, emerging markets, strategic initiatives, corporate restructuring, enterprise information technology infrastructure composition and requirements, intra-company production and development methodologies (Six-Sigma, Agile, Waterfall, Scrum).
- Manage database information and use enterprise content management system to publish quarterly custom market research reports on more than 100 Fortune 1000 companies in dozens of industries.
- Analyze SEC filings, annual reports, quarterly reports, corporate finances and earnings calls.
- Track corporate capital expenditures, with an emphasis on IT software and hardware expenditures.
- Research financial and information technology trends on enterprise- and industry-wide scale.
- Maintain, purge and regularly update relational databases containing several million data points.
- Collaborated with QA team to perform quality assurance testing of custom news aggregator product.

Advocates, Inc.
Direct Care Counselor / Health Record Coordinator (May 2013 – December 2013)
- Helped patients navigate legal and mental health systems.
- Designed and implemented mental health treatment plans.
- Advised patients on methods of achieving financial and social independence.
- Evaluated patients for psychological symptoms and effectiveness of prescribed medication.
- Managed patient health record and rehabilitation database.

Rockland County, New York Courthouse
Judicial Intern to The Honorable Judge William Nelson (Summer 2012)
- Shadowed Judge Nelson through criminal trials and hearings, and in meetings with assistant district attorneys and criminal defense attorneys.
- Performed legal research and advised the judge on relevant matters of case law pertaining to current cases.
- Analyzed courtroom proceedings with Judge Nelson, his principal law clerk, attorneys and other interns.
- Proofread legal motions and briefs.
- Facilitated communication between the Judge Nelson and other judges, clerks and attorneys.

Sample 2.4

After

Edited resume of Matthew Novack (2–3 years experience).

---

① Matthew T. Novack
③ (845) 123-4567 mtnovack@wustl.edu **④**

Permanent Address: **②**
16 Adams Court, Nanuet, NY 10954

School Address:
7025 Forsyth Dr., St. Louis, MO 63105

EDUCATION
Washington University School of Law, JD Candidate   *May 2018*
Honors and Activities
- Recipient: Scholar in Law (merit-based XX% tuition scholarship for three years)
- Recipient: William R. and Nancy J. Hirsch Scholarship (merit-based XX% tuition scholarship for three years)
- 1L Elected Representative: IP Law Society
- 1L Appointed Representative: Employment Law Society
- Participant: Client Counseling & Interviewing Competition
- Member: Negotiation and Dispute Resolution Society

Boston University, B.A., Psychology   *May 2013*
Honors and Activities
- Dean's List
- Member: Kappa Sigma Fraternity
- Member: Sigma Alpha Lambda Honor Society

LAW-RELATED EXPERIENCE
Office of Frederick Winsmann, PhD, Clinical and Forensic Psychologist, Boston, Massachusetts.
Forensic Psychology Research Assistant   *March 2014 – Present*
Research and analyze criminal and behavioral patterns using legal, medical, and personal records for use in forensic reports to help evaluate criminal responsibility, risk of reoffending, competency to stand trial, and SVP civil commitment. Draft sections of forensic reports for submission to federal and state courts. Review and incorporate legal documents and research statutes pertaining to mental health commitment and competency to stand trial. Adhere to strict industry standards of quality and confidentiality. File trademark application with USPTO for continuing education symposium on psychology and the law.

Rockland County District Court, New City, New York.
Judicial Intern   *Summer 2012*
Observed criminal trials and hearings, and meetings between assistant district attorneys, defense attorneys, and judges. Performed basic legal research and discussed relevant matters of case law pertaining to current cases with judge. Relayed information between judges, clerks, and attorneys.

BUSINESS EXPERIENCE
Avention, Inc. (Formerly OneSource Information Services – 200+ employees), Concord, Massachusetts.
Market Research Analyst   *March 2014–August 2015*
Researched and analyzed competitive intelligence information including corporate strategy and risk, research and development expenditures, emerging markets, strategic initiatives, corporate restructuring, enterprise information technology infrastructure composition and requirements, intra-company production and development methodologies (Six-Sigma, Agile, Waterfall, Scrum). Analyzed SEC filings, annual reports, quarterly reports, corporate finances and earnings calls. Researched financial and information technology trends on enterprise- and industry-wide scale. Tracked corporate capital expenditures with an emphasis on IT software and hardware expenditures. Maintained, purged, and regularly updated database information. Used enterprise content management system to publish quarterly custom market research reports on more than 100 Fortune 1000 companies in dozens of industries.

OTHER PROFESSIONAL EXPERIENCE
Advocates, Inc., Dedham, Massachusetts.

Direct Care Counselor   *May 2013–December 2013*
Assisted in the design and implementation of individualized mental health treatment plans. Helped evaluate patients for psychological symptoms and effectiveness of prescribed medication.

INTERESTS: Boating, swimming, wakeboarding, waterskiing, snowboarding, and playing guitar.

Notes:

1. No changes are needed to his name.

2. Matthew added his permanent address to show a connection to his target area, New York.

3. He has changed his outgoing voicemail message to sound more professional. Matthew checks his voice mail at least twice a day to make sure he has not missed an Employer's message.

4. Matthew is using his law school email.

Sample 2.5

Before

Resume of Stacy Stevens (more than 3 years experience).

Notes:

1. Even though the font is large, Stacy's name should be at the top of her resume and not under other identifying information. She needs to add her middle initial if she has one.

2. Stacy needs to update her resume to include her law school address.

3. Stacy's cell phone number is fine. However, she needs to add her area code. It is not necessary to include the word "CELL."

4. Stacy needs to use her law school email and not her Yahoo account.

② 123 SMITHTON ST. • LAPLACE, LA 70068
④ STACYSTEVENS@YAHOO.COM • 123-4567 (CELL) **③**
① STACY STEVENS

EDUCATION & HONORS

Rice University, Houston, TX   August 2007-May 2011
Bachelor of Arts in Sociology awarded on: May 14, 2011 (GPA: X.XX/4.00)
- **Magna Cum Laude**
- **Phi Beta Kappa**
- President's Honor Roll: *Maintained a GPA that was in the top 30% of undergraduates*
- Leadership Rice Summer Mentorship Experience Fellow
- Pre-Law Undergraduate Scholars (PLUS) Outstanding Student at UNL-Law Program

University of Paris IV- Sorbonne, Paris, France   Spring 2010
Completed a study abroad program that focused on French language, history, and culture

EXPERIENCE

The World Race   Asia, Europe, Africa
Logistics Coordinator   September 2013-August 2014
- Traveled to 11 countries in the span of 11 months as part of a missionary team
- Partnered with local organizations and ministries to serve the community and address social issues
- Led efforts to teach English, clean dumpsites, host children's camps, restore buildings, and distribute food
- Coordinated transportation, lodging, and administration for 40+ people

Jackson Elementary School   Jackson, LA
*Second Grade Teacher with **Teach for America***   July 2011-July 2013
- Developed over 20 lessons and activities per week, created resources, presented content on various topics
- Facilitated student growth of over 1.8 years in reading
- Managed 17 students in behavior and character development and addressed special needs a on case-by-case basis

Rice University Faculty Club   Houston, TX
Banquet Server/Waitress   January 2008-May 2011
- Facilitated satisfaction of over 150 customers through fulfillment of orders and resolution of complaints
- Improved atmosphere of facilities and maintained order of resources and supplies

The Impact Movement   Orlando, FL
Assistant to Director of Communications   Summer 2010
- Published a promotional article in two newspapers and forged a partnership between two organizations
- Redesigned marketing strategies and produced conference material for over 1500 attendees

U. S. Equal Employment Opportunity Commission   Houston, TX
Legal Intern/Mentee   Summer 2009
- Designed a large applicant database of over 300 contacts and located possible witnesses
- Conducted research on case facts and witness history and analyzed legal writings for accuracy
- Shadowed the lead attorney for his leadership abilities and completed leadership profiles of managers

ACTIVITIES

- Impact Movement, Conference Planner (2011-2012)
- Impact Movement, President (2007-2011)
- Black Student Union, Service Chair (2007-2011)
- Professional Development Advisor (2009-2011)
- Advocating Diversity Association (2008-2011)
- Melodious Voices Gospel Choir (2007-2011)
- Jones College Powderpuff Team (2007-2011)
- Leadership Rice Mentorship Experience (Summer 2009)
- Pre-Law Undergraduate Scholars (Summer 2008)

CERTIFICATIONS & SKILLS

- Certified teacher in Louisiana for grades 1-5 (2012-2015)
- Speak Intermediate French, write basic French, and speak basic Spanish

After

Edited resume of Stacy Stevens (more than 3 years experience).

7345 Yale Ave. Apt 2E ②
St. Louis, MO 63130

④ stacyastevens@wustl.edu
③ 504-123-4567

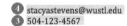 ① **Stacy A. Stevens**

EDUCATION

Washington University School of Law St. Louis, Missouri
J.D. Candidate May 2018
Honors and Activities
- Recipient - Dean's Fellowship ($X tuition for three years, faculty mentor, research assistantship)
- Finalist - 1L Client Counseling Competition (one of 24 teams out of 72 participating)
- Member - Women's Law Caucus - Auction Committee Member (largest student-led fundraiser designated for 2L public interest summer stipend)
- Member - Public Service Advisory Board-Public Service Committee; Black Law Students Association; International Law Society

Rice University Houston, Texas
Bachelor of Arts in Sociology, magna cum laude (GPA: X.XX/4.00) May 2011
Honors and Activities
- Inductee - *Phi Beta Kappa*
- Recipient - QuestBridge Scholarship ($X tuition and living expenses for four years)
- President - The Impact Movement (Rice chapter of national org.) - collaborated with Asst. Dean for Students to plan initiatives, drafted proposals for organization funding, served as liaison between campus and national organization, spearheaded on-campus outreach, and coordinated logistics for national conference
- Community Service Chair - Black Students Association (elected position) - coordinated community events
- Member - Advocating Diversity Association - Event Committee Member - secured sponsorship from local businesses, obtained funding from student government, and allocated facilities for program use

PUBLIC SERVICE & NON-PROFIT EXPERIENCE

The World Race Asia, Europe, Africa
Participant and Logistics Coordinator (appointed position) September 2013-August 2014
Traveled to 11 countries in 11 months as part of missionary team; raised $15,500 in funds through presentations and letters to board members and individual investors; partnered with local organizations and ministries to combat human trafficking, teach English, feed and clothe orphans, clean townships, and restore buildings; coordinated transportation, lodging, and administration for 40+ people; and served as liaison between on-site team and headquarters' logistics leader.

The Impact Movement Orlando, FL
Assistant to Director of Communications Summer 2010
Drafted promotional article for *The Orlando Times* to publicize organization; coordinated regular publishing opportunities for organization; redesigned marketing strategies; and developed conference materials for 1500 attendees.

LEGALLY RELATED EXPERIENCE

U. S. Equal Employment Opportunity Commission Houston, TX
Legal Intern/Mentee Summer 2009
Conducted research on case facts and witness history; reviewed legal memos and briefs for accuracy; attended witness deposition; shadowed director of district office; designed applicant database of over 300 contacts; and located witnesses.

TEACHING EXPERIENCE

Teach for America - Jackson Elementary School Jackson, LA
Second Grade Teacher July 2011-July 2013
Developed over 20 lessons and activities per week; facilitated student growth of 1.8 years in reading; managed 17 students in behavior and character development; created specialized plan for student needs; forged critical parent and student relationships in furtherance of common goal; and campaigned for county-wide tax initiative to benefit students.

St. Charles Parish Schools Destrehan, LA
Substitute Teacher August 2014-May 2015
Assisted special education students in schoolwork and recreation activities; completed individualized student plans and tracking charts; and coordinated with parents to implement student-specific goals.

SKILLS & INTERESTS

Languages: French (Limited Working Proficiency) and Spanish (Elementary Proficiency)
Alto - Gospel Choir

Notes:

1. Stacy's name is centered and stands alone so that it is prominent. She added her middle initial like attorneys do.

2. Because Stacy is not targeting a particular city for her job search, she has only included her law school address.

3. Stacy added her area code. She has checked her voicemail message to make sure that it sounds professional, and that there is no background noise or music.

4. Stacy is now using her official law school email and checks it at least twice a day for emails from Employers.

Sample 2.6

Checklist: Identifying Information

Name:	Yes	No
Did you use your legal name?		
Did you include your middle initial?		
If you are an international student, did you include an American name in addition to your given name?		
If you are an international student and you want the Employer to know your gender, did you include an honorific (Mr., Ms., or Mx.)?		
Address:		
Did you include your law school address and label it as such?		
If you included an additional address to show a connection to a target city, did you label it as a "Permanent" or "Home" address?		
If you are an international student seeking employment outside the U.S., did you include an address in that target country and city?		
If you included an address in addition to your law school address, did you notify a resident at that address that you are using it?		
Phone Number:		
Did you include a phone number for which you regularly answer and check messages?		
Did you check to make sure your voicemail is working properly?		
Do you have a professional-sounding message as your voicemail?		
Does the name on your voicemail message match the name on your resume?		
Have you deleted all background noises, including music, from your voicemail message?		
Do you check your voicemail at least twice a day for messages?		
Email:		
Did you include your law school email address?		
Did you exclude your Gmail or other email address?		
Do you check your law school email at least twice a day for messages?		
On all outgoing emails, do you have an automatic professional signature block that includes your name, law school, degree and year of expected graduation, phone number, LinkedIn link, and law school logo?		
Proofing:		
Is the font consistent with the rest of your resume (although your name may be slightly larger)?		
Is this section formatted consistently with the rest of your resume?		
Are there any proofing errors (misspelled words, incorrect punctuation, etc.)?		

Chapter 3

Education: Where Did You Go to School and What Did You Do While You Were There?

Purpose of Section

Employers look for two qualities in law students: 1) intelligence (academic achievement that shows you are smart enough for sophisticated legal work); and 2) professional skills (demonstrated leadership and transferable skills from work or other experiences that will contribute to your success as an attorney). The "Education" section of your resume speaks most directly to the first quality Employers seek: intelligence.

Step-by-Step Guide

Names, Location of Schools, and Dates of Graduation or Attendance

As a law student, begin this section of your resume with your legal education. The order is law school first, graduate, and then undergraduate school. Even if you went to a well-known, selective high school, take that information off your resume. If you are thinking, "But my high school is well known in the city I want to practice in," you can still use the benefits of that connection by including, for example, your participation in your high school alumni association in a "Community Involvement" section further down in your resume. (We will discuss how to do this in future chapters.) Identify your law school, graduate school, and undergraduate school each by its full name and city. Consider putting your school's location to the far right of your resume; this gets an Employer's attention, creates a connection to that city, and shows a trail of places where you have studied or worked. Date of graduation, or attendance if you did not graduate from a particular school, go under the city. (Examples will be found at the end of this chapter.)

Degrees, Latin Honors, and Grades
Degrees

Be accurate and specific when listing your degree. There is a big difference between a B.A. and a B.F.A., and a B.S. and a B.A., and you may have to look back at your records or diploma to get this one right. If your school had majors and minors, include those as well. For this resume draft, and at this stage of your employment exploration, include as much information as possible. Majors and minors can give Employers something to discuss with you in interviews. Also, if you have two degrees from one university — undergraduate and graduate — list them separately if space permits.

Latin Honors

If you graduated with Latin honors such as *cum laude, magna cum laude,* or *summa cum laude,* include them in italics right after your degree. (Where and how to include other honors, including departmental honors, will be explained below.)

Grades

Many students wonder whether they should include their GPA on their resume. This is a great question to ask your law school career advisor, as he or she will know what Employers expect in your target market. The short answer is probably, but it depends. For our purposes, let's assume that it is best to include your GPA. This means that before grades are released for your first semester of law school, you will only have your undergraduate and graduate grades available. That is often good news for law students, as you have done well academically or you would not be in law school reading this book.

There are several ways to convey your GPA on a resume. One way is to include it for your entire school experience. (If you include your GPA for your undergraduate and other degrees, you need to include it for your legal education, as well.) However, following the principles of persuasive legal writing, you'll want to frame your GPA as positively as possible. This means that if your major or minor GPA is higher than your overall GPA, you should also include those GPAs.

Stating your law school GPA in a persuasive manner applies slightly differently. As a 1L, you will have a limited number of grades at the end of first semester. Therefore, if you have done well in a particular course, you could highlight that grade separately, especially if you are interested in a re-lated practice area. For example, if you did exceptionally well in Contracts and are interested in employment law, it makes sense to highlight that course grade, as employment law involves contracts. When you include that Contracts grade, it would also be important to show where that grade stands in the academic ranking. If your Contracts grade was a 3.8 or A- and that is the top 10%, you could include this on your resume: "Contracts — 3.8 (top 10%)." For better or worse, Employers want to know where you stand compared to your classmates. This is exactly why we have the mandatory curve grading system most students (and faculty!) dislike; Employers want it. Most faculty can give students an idea of where their grade is in comparison to peers (top 10 %, etc.); ask your professor for that information.

If you have done well in your legal writing and/or research course (LRW) specifically, you should absolutely emphasize that grade, as all Employers are looking for law students who can research and write. However, even if your final grade is not a high one, your LRW professor may still have wonderful things to say about you to an Employer. I routinely serve as a reference for students who have not done as well as they had hoped to do in my course. I can speak about the student's work ethic, teamwork, intellectual curiosity, professional skills, and many other qualities Employers are looking for, and I often tell them when I am confident about a student's potential and don't believe the course grade reflects that student's abilities. At this stage of your legal career, it is important to understand that many skills go into being a great attorney, and they are learned over time.

Significant Writing and Publications

If you wrote a thesis in undergraduate or graduate school, include it on your resume with its title and date. This shows an Employer that you have accomplished a significant research and writing project — research and writing is what attorneys do every day — and also gives you something to talk about in an interview. Sometimes a thesis might be on a controversial topic that wouldn't be appropriate for a legal resume, but this is rare. Double-check with your law school career advisor. The title of your thesis should be included in italics right under your degree or as part of the next section, "Honors and Activities," unless it was published. Include any publications in a section called "Publications" right under "Education," and use an appropriate citation format. Sometimes students are provided with a citation for the paper by the journal that published it; if you are not sure what the appropriate citation format is, use the Bluebook. (This shows an Employer that you are familiar with the professional standard.)

Licenses and Certifications

If you have a license that is relevant to a legal job, include it in this section. Generally, a relevant license is one that you have earned by examination. For example, if you are a Certified Public Accountant (CPA), and are interested in corporate, financial, or any kind of business practice, this information would be relevant. If you are a licensed professional engineer (PE), that license is relevant to real estate or environmental law. Securities licenses earned by examination are also relevant to legal practice. For these, include the exam name and date you passed: for example, "Series 79 — (Date Passed)." Even though your license may have lapsed since entering law school, the fact that you passed that exam signals to an Employer that you understand securities and securities regulations. It also tells an Employer that you are intelligent, as these exams are challenging. If you are submitting your resume to an Employer that does not specialize in securities or financial services law, include the type of security covered by the exam: e.g., "Series 79 (Investment Banking Representative Examination)." Once you pass the bar, include your bar membership by state, year, and perhaps court under the category "Bar Memberships" rather than "Licenses." While you are in school, the term "Licenses" is more appropriate.

With all licenses or certifications, include an explanation of the acronym if it is not universally known. While most people have heard of a CPA, you may not know what a CFA (Chartered Financial Analyst) is unless you are in the financial field. Similar to descriptions of scholarships (see below), an Employer must understand an acronym or the purpose of including it is lost.

Honors

When listing your honors and activities, you'll want to follow two of the tenets of effective legal writing: "Best goes first," and "Focus on the subject" (you!). List the most prestigious honor first. If you are fortunate enough to receive a scholarship, include that in "Honors." This is true whether or not your scholarship is merit- or need-based. A scholarship signals to an Employer that you are so smart your law school or college paid for you to attend. Even if your scholarship is need-based, you did not receive it without significant academic achievement; it just comes from a different line item in your law school's budget.

When listing scholarships, be very specific and keep the focus on you. Start with the word "Recipient." Next, include the formal name of the scholarship (this adds to its prestige; many scholarships are named for donors) and an explanation of its nature, including the amount or percent of tuition the scholarship covers. For some of you, this means that you will have to do some research; go back through your records or contact your school's financial aid or admissions office. If you are applying for jobs in your law school's city and your scholarship is named for a prominent member of that community, the scholarship name adds another connection between you and that community.

Other types of honors often included are membership in major well-known honor societies, like *Phi Beta Kappa*, departmental honors, membership in honor societies for different disciplines, and inclusion on a Dean's List. If you are a member of *Phi Beta Kappa,* that should be listed first, since it is so well recognized. For all honors, first name your role rather than the honor. For example, "Inductee — *Phi Beta Kappa*" works well because the word "Inductee" places the emphasis on you, where you want it to be. If you graduated with departmental honors, include an explanation (such as "Recipient — Psychology Departmental Honors (top 10% of graduates)") right after you list the honor. Employers cannot possibly be familiar with the honors system of every university, so this description makes it easier for them to see your accomplishments. Other honors typically included are book awards, awards for best paper, and Dean's List. With Dean's List honors, include the specific semesters you received such honor or the number of semesters (e.g., "7/8 semesters").

Activities

This section of your resume serves one of the purposes mentioned at the beginning of this chapter: showing Employers that you have the intelligence and the professional skills to do the work they do.

When including activities in which you are or were involved at your school, make strategic choices. "Best goes first" means leading with activities in which you played a significant role or had an elected or appointed position. For example, if you are an elected representative to the Student Bar Association, you would include something like "1L Elected Representative — Student Bar Association." The fact that you were elected means that you were chosen for the position; you did not just sign up for it. In describing your duties or positions in an organization, highlight professional skills that would be assets for legal employment. For example, if you were a treasurer of a fraternity or sorority, include the budget numbers. Something like "Treasurer — Greek Week (managed budget >$10,000)" shows significant responsibility. Another significant position might be a teaching assistantship, which typically involves research, writing, and communication — things attorneys do consistently. Serving as a teaching assistant for a course that teaches these skills shows that you excel in them. Depending on your role in a particular organization and the depth of your work with that group, you might include that activity under work experience rather than in "Education."

Bottom line: when deciding which activities to include on your resume, think of *why* those activities might be relevant. Sometimes they can be used to show a connection to a field of practice or affinity group that could be important to an Employer. For example, if you are involved in international law groups or public interest law organizations and you want to practice in those areas, it would be important to emphasize those associations. Another example is involvement in an affinity group like the LGBTQ Student Law Society, Black Law Students Association, or Jewish Law Students, especially if you are interested in an area of law like civil rights.

Additional Tips for International Students:

Undergraduate School

Unless an Employer is familiar with your university, you may want to include additional information, such as a national or international ranking, that indicates the caliber of your institution. One system that Employers are likely to be familiar with is the "Best Global Universities Ranking" published yearly by *U.S. News & World Report — Education.* Use the highest ranking for your university whether it is by country or by world, and include it in parentheses next to the name of your university. This would look something like: *"Peking University (#2 Best Global Universities in Asia — U.S. News & World Report)"* rather than *"(#31 Best Global Universities — U.S. News & World Report)."*

GPA

If your GPA is not determined on the 4.0 scale typical for U.S. universities, one option is to convert it to the 4.0 scale and note that it was converted. There are several conversion calculators available online to calculate GPA using country-specific grading systems. Another option is to note your ranking in your class, if your university ranks students, rather than your GPA. A third is to include your international GPA with an explanation noting the relative strength of your GPA to other students in your university or major.

Visas and Work Permits

If you are studying in the U.S. on a student visa, you may or may not have a temporary work permit. Employers must know if you have permission to work in the U.S.; therefore, it is helpful to create an additional category under the "Education" section that notes the type of visa you have for study and for work. If you have U.S. citizenship, you will not need to provide this information.

Chapter 3

Sample Resumes

Education

Sample 3.1

Before

Resume of Laura Mackey (0–1 year experience).

Notes:

1. Laura includes each of the universities she attended and the dates of attendance. She needs to add her degrees from UC–Riverside and her law school.

2. Laura's achievements and honors would be more noticeable if included for each school and with an explanation of the significance of each honor.

3. Laura's activities should likewise be included under the appropriate school.

Laura Mary Mackey
1234 Canyon Ridge Dr. #109 Riverside, CA 92507
laura.m.mackey@gmail.com
805.123.4567

Education

❶ | **University of California, Riverside** | **2013-Present**
Major: Political Science, Law and Society
GPA: X.XX

Santa Barbara City College | **2008- 2013**
Associates Degree: Political Science, Liberal Arts
Major: Political Science
GPA: X.XX

Boston University | **2007-2008**
Major: Biology

Work Experience

United States Pretrial Services | **January 2014-June 2014**
Intern
- Assisted Officers during court proceedings
- Observed Pretrial interviews and report processes

Santa Barbara Superior Court | **October 2011-August 2013**
Own Recognizance Investigator
- Began as an intern/volunteer and was promoted to paid Judicial Assistant II
- Interview inmates and prepare reports for the Judges to determine the defendant's custody status
- Work as a liaison between the Court and local arresting agencies
- Help inmates and their friends/family understand and navigate the legal process

Santa Barbara City College Internship | **April 2013**
Political Science Department
- Observed and interacted with numerous lawmakers in Sacramento to gain a deeper understanding of state-level politics

Jackson Medical Group | **October 2008- June 2012**
Billing Assistant
- Submitted patients' visits to insurance companies.
- Helped disgruntled patients frustrated with the medical billing process
- Deposited and balanced insurance payments

❷ **Achievements**
President's Honor List | **2012**
Santa Barbara City College

Chancellor's Honor List | **2013-2014**
University of California, Riverside

Dean's Academic Distinction Award | **2014**
University of California, Riverside

Pi Sigma Alpha Member | **Spring 2014-Present**
Political Science Honors Society
University of California, Riverside

❸ **Extracurricular Involvement**
Mock Trial | **2013-Present**
University of California, Riverside
- Vice President

Foreign Language
Spanish
- Reading, Comprehension and Writing: Advanced
- Speaking: Intermediate

After

Edited resume of Laura Mackey (0–1 year experience).

Notes:

Laura Mary Mackey

123 Westgate Ave #6
St. Louis, MO 63130

805.123.4567
lmm@wustl.edu

Education

❶ Washington University School of Law — **St. Louis, MO**
J.D. Candidate — May 2018
❷ Honors and Activities
    Recipient: Scholar of Law Scholarship (merit-based, $X/year for 3 years)
    Member: Women's Law Caucus; American Constitution Society
    Participant: Client Counseling Competition

❶ University of California, Riverside — **Riverside, CA**
B.A., Political Science, Law and Society, *summa cum laude* — June 2015
❷ Honors and Activities
    Recipient: Dean's Honor List (3 consecutive quarters with GPA of at least X.X) and Dean's Academic
      Distinction Award (required GPA of at least X.X)
    Vice President (elected position, 2014-2015); member (2013-2015) - Mock Trial
      As Vice President team won Honorable Mention at local competition (1st time for UCR). Worked with team
      members to improve direct and cross-examination questions and techniques. Organized and ran practices.

❶ Santa Barbara City College — **Santa Barbara, CA**
A.A., Political Science — May 2013
❷   Recipient: President's Honor List (required GPA of at least X.X)

Boston University — **Boston, MA**
May 2008

Legally Related Experience

United States Pretrial Services — **Riverside, CA**
Intern — January 2014-June 2014
    Observed U.S. Pretrial Officers during initial bail hearings, bail reviews, and inmate interviews. Verified
    criminal records. Coordinated inmate intake with federal agencies including FBI, DEA, U.S. Marshals.

Santa Barbara Superior Court — **Santa Barbara, CA**
Own Recognizance Investigator — October 2011-August 2013
    Began as an intern and promoted to paid Judicial Assistant II within four months. Interviewed inmates at county
    jail and drafted custody status reports for judges. Reviewed inmates' prior criminal records. Reviewed Probable
    Cause Declarations and submitted to judges. Completed bail increase/reduction documents and release
    paperwork and submitted documents to custody officers. Researched Los Angeles County bail schedule. Served
    as liaison between Court and sheriff's department, police department, probation officers, and parole officers.
    Assisted inmates and their friends/family in understanding and navigating the legal process.

Other Professional Experience

Jackson Medical Group — **Santa Barbara, CA**
(General Practice Group with 12 physicians in 4 offices)
Billing Assistant — October 2008-June 2012
    Submitted records of patients' visits to insurance companies. Deposited and balanced insurance payments.
    Worked with major national insurance companies such as Blue Cross, Blue Shield, Cigna, and AARP as well as
    Medicare. All tasks complied with HIPAA regulations. Assisted patients in resolving conflicts with insurance
    companies.

Interests
    Ran two marathons. Hiked Mt. Whitney (14,509 ft., highest mountain in contiguous United States).

Foreign Language
    Spanish
        Speaking: Limited Working Proficiency. Reading: Limited Working Proficiency.

1. Laura added her law school and the degree expected. She also added the degrees and Latin Honors she earned from each school.

2. Her honors and activities are listed high on her resume so that they can be more noticeable. Each honor and activity is included under the school in which she received it. To describe an honor or activity, Laura started with a noun such as "Recipient," to keep the focus on her. She added an explanation of the honors and activities as needed.

Sample 3.3

Before

Resume of Carrie Yu (2–3 years experience).

Notes:

1. Carrie lists the schools she attended, including their locations and dates of attendance. It is difficult to see them, however, as they are not in the far right margin. She received honors at her undergraduate school but has not listed them properly. She also needs to add her law school.

2. Carrie includes her activities as related to each school. However, she lists the name of the group first and not her position within the group. This puts the emphasis on the group instead of on her.

Carrie Yu
123 Lexington Avenue 2S New York NY 10016 | (703) 123-4567 | YuCarrie@gmail.com

EDUCATION

① **GEORGETOWN UNIVERSITY**, Washington, DC
Bachelor of Arts in Government and Psychology, *with honors*, received May 2013 (GPA: X.XX)

② Thesis: *The Effect of the Addition of a Semantically Meaningful Context and Language on the Video Deficit Effect*
Activities: Class of 2013 Committee, Secretary
Builder for Habitat for Humanity and The Fuller House Foundation
Georgetown College Peer Advisor

① **UNIVERSITY COLLEGE LONDON**, London, England
Semester Abroad Spring 2012

EXPERIENCE

PAUL, WEISS, RIFKIND, WHARTON & GARRISON LLP, New York, NY
Litigation Paralegal, June 2013 – Present
- Prepared documents for deposition and trial in connection with a multibillion dollar civil case
- Managed and supervised team of 30 other paralegals on a foreclosure case

GEORGETOWN UNIVERSITY EARLY LEARNING PROJECT, Washington, DC
Undergraduate Research Assistant, January 2011 – May 2013
- Conducted research on early childhood learning from television and touchscreens
- Co-authored a poster presented at the International Conference on Infant Studies, in Minneapolis in June 2012, titled "The Effects of Instructions on Imitation from Live and Video Demonstrations"

GEORGETOWN UNIVERSITY GOVERNMENT DEPARTMENT, Washington, DC
Undergraduate Research Assistant, September 2012 – December 2012
- Researched and drafted profiles on states' sex education policies for a professor who is writing a book

WILDWOOD SUMMER THEATER, Bethesda, MD
Director of Fundraising, June 2012 – August 2012
- Headed the fundraising efforts of a 501(c)(3) theater company, raising $20,000

UNIVERSITY COLLEGE LONDON DEPARTMENT OF PSYCHOLOGY, London, England
Undergraduate Research Assistant, January 2012 – May 2012
- Recruited participants, collected and analyzed data that examined how people from collectivist cultures and individualistic cultures view the idea of power
- Authored an Independent Research Study titled *Culture, Power, and Inhibition: An Examination of the Effects of Power on Inhibition in Asian Populations*

GEORGETOWN UNIVERSITY WRITING CENTER, Washington, DC
Writing Tutor and English Teaching Assistant, September 2010 – May 2011
- Assisted English professors in their introductory English classes; read and revised undergraduate and graduate students' papers, advising them on how they can improve their writing

SPIRIT FOUNDATION, Rockville, MD
Board Member, May 2010 – May 2011
- Fundraised for an annual $5000 college scholarship for a graduating high school senior
- Planned and managed the award banquet – attended by over 100 people – celebrating the SPIRIT Foundation scholarship winner (May 2011)

INTEREST & SKILLS

Musical Theater ◆ Level 6 Pianist ◆ Photography ◆ Paul Weiss Volleyball Team ◆ Running ◆ Fluent in Chinese

Sample 3.4

After

Edited resume of Carrie Yu (2–3 years experience).

Carrie S.Yu
12 South Kingshighway Blvd., Apt. 12S, St. Louis, MO 63108 | (703) 123-4567 | carriesyu@wustl.edu

EDUCATION

① **WASHINGTON UNIVERSITY SCHOOL OF LAW**   St. Louis, MO
J.D. Candidate   May 2018
② Honors: Scholar in Law Award (merit-based $X tuition scholarship for all three years)
    Activities: 1L Representative – Asian Pacific American Law Students Association
                  Member – Women's Law Caucus
                  Participant – 1L Client Counseling Competition

① **GEORGETOWN UNIVERSITY**   Washington, DC
B.A., majors in Government and Psychology, *cum laude*   May 2013
② Honors: Psychology Departmental Honors
    Thesis: *The Effect of the Addition of a Semantically Meaningful Context & Language on the Video Deficit Effect*
    Activities: Secretary – Class of 2013 Committee
                  Member – Habitat for Humanity (3 years)
                  Member – College Peer Advisors (2 years)

① **UNIVERSITY COLLEGE LONDON**   London, England
Semester Abroad (including significant research and writing courses culminating in thesis)   Spring 2012
② Thesis: *Culture, Power, and Inhibition: An Examination of the Effect of Power on Inhibition in Asian Populations*

PUBLICATIONS & PRESENTATIONS

③ • Zimmermann L, Moser A, Grenell A, Dickerson K, Yao Q, Gerhardstein P and Barr R (2015) Do semantic contextual cues facilitate transfer learning from video in toddlers? *Front. Psychol.* 6:561. doi:10.3389/fpsyg.2015.00561
 • Dickerson K, Oot E, Yao Q, Barr R, Gerhardstein P (2012) *The effect of instructions on imitation from live and video demonstrations.* Poster presentation at the International Conference on Infant Studies, Minneapolis MN

LEGAL EXPERIENCE
PAUL, WEISS, RIFKIND, WHARTON & GARRISON LLP   New York, NY
Litigation Paralegal   June 2013–July 2015
 • Supervised and managed team of 30 paralegals, as lead paralegal, of foreclosure case.
 • Conducted research and prepared documents for filings, depositions, hearings, and trial, for nine-month, multi-billion dollar environmental damages trial.

SIGNIFICANT RESEARCH AND WRITING EXPERIENCE
GEORGETOWN UNIVERSITY EARLY LEARNING PROJECT   Washington, DC
Undergraduate Psychology Research Assistant   Jan 2011–May 2013
 • Collected and analyzed data on early childhood learning from television and touchscreens.

GEORGETOWN UNIVERSITY GOVERNMENT DEPARTMENT   Washington, DC
Undergraduate Government Research Assistant   Sept 2012–Dec 2012
 • Drafted memos on multi-state policies regarding abstinence-only sex education.

GEORGETOWN UNIVERSITY WRITING CENTER   Washington, DC
Writing Tutor and English Teaching Assistant (Competitive Selection) Sept 2010–May 2011
 • Read and revised undergraduate and graduate students' papers. Recommended improvements to students' writing.

COMMUNITY ENGAGEMENT
WILDWOOD SUMMER THEATER   Bethesda, MD
Director of Fundraising   June 2012–Aug 2012
 • Headed the fundraising efforts of 501c(3) theater company and exceeded fundraising goal of $20,000.

SPIRIT FOUNDATION (Scholarship Foundation Founded in Memory of High School Classmate)   Rockville, MD
Board Member   May 2010–May 2011
 • Fundraised for annual $5000 college scholarship for graduating high school senior.

SPECIAL SKILLS & INTERESTS
Chinese (Fluent) ◆ Level 6 Pianist ◆ Photography (Winner of Online Contests) ◆ Firm Volleyball Team ◆ Musical Theater Enthusiast

Notes:

1. Carrie has added her law school. Her Latin Honors are now listed appropriately. Carrie added an explanation of her study abroad, which amplifies the significance of that experience.

2. Carrie began the explanation of her honors and activities by focusing on her role. She included an explanation of each when appropriate and the number of years of her involvement.

3. Carrie included her publications and presentations as a separate category, which makes them more prominent. She used proper citation format for each one.

Sample 3.5

Before

Resume of Stacy Stevens (more than 3 years experience).

Notes:

1. Stacy lists each school she attended, her degrees, GPA, and the dates of her attendance. It is not necessary to list the actual date of graduation.

2. She received two very high honors — *magna cum laude* and *Phi Beta Kappa* — but they are not listed in the proper format. Stacy's activities are at the bottom of her resume in no particular order, which makes them seem less important.

3. Stacy lists her teacher certification, but because it was only for a limited amount of time, has expired, and is not relevant to the legal internship she is seeking, it is not necessary.

---

123 SMITHTON ST. • LAPLACE, LA 70068
STACYSTEVENS@YAHOO.COM • 123-4567 (CELL)
STACY STEVENS

EDUCATION & HONORS

(1) Rice University, Houston, TX — August 2007-May 2011
Bachelor of Arts in Sociology awarded on: May 14, 2011 (GPA: X.XX/4.00)

(2)
- **Magna Cum Laude**
- **Phi Beta Kappa**
- President's Honor Roll: *Maintained a GPA that was in the top 30% of undergraduates*
- Leadership Rice Summer Mentorship Experience Fellow
- Pre-Law Undergraduate Scholars (PLUS) Outstanding Student at UNL-Law Program

(1) University of Paris IV- Sorbonne, Paris, France — Spring 2010
Completed a study abroad program that focused on French language, history, and culture

EXPERIENCE

The World Race — Asia, Europe, Africa
Logistics Coordinator — September 2013-August 2014
- Traveled to 11 countries in the span of 11 months as part of a missionary team
- Partnered with local organizations and ministries to serve the community and address social issues
- Led efforts to teach English, clean dumpsites, host children's camps, restore buildings, and distribute food
- Coordinated transportation, lodging, and administration for 40+ people

Jackson Elementary School — Jackson, LA
Second Grade Teacher with Teach for America — July 2011-July 2013
- Developed over 20 lessons and activities per week, created resources, presented content on various topics
- Facilitated student growth of over 1.8 years in reading
- Managed 17 students in behavior and character development and addressed special needs a on case-by-case basis

Rice University Faculty Club — Houston, TX
Banquet Server/Waitress — January 2008-May 2011
- Facilitated satisfaction of over 150 customers through fulfillment of orders and resolution of complaints
- Improved atmosphere of facilities and maintained order of resources and supplies

The Impact Movement — Orlando, FL
Assistant to Director of Communications — Summer 2010
- Published a promotional article in two newspapers and forged a partnership between two organizations
- Redesigned marketing strategies and produced conference material for over 1500 attendees

U. S. Equal Employment Opportunity Commission — Houston, TX
Legal Intern/Mentee — Summer 2009
- Designed a large applicant database of over 300 contacts and located possible witnesses
- Conducted research on case facts and witness history and analyzed legal writings for accuracy
- Shadowed the lead attorney for his leadership abilities and completed leadership profiles of managers

ACTIVITIES

(2)
- Impact Movement, Conference Planner (2011-2012)
- Impact Movement, President (2007-2011)
- Black Student Union, Service Chair (2007-2011)
- Professional Development Advisor (2009-2011)
- Advocating Diversity Association (2008-2011)
- Melodious Voices Gospel Choir (2007-2011)
- Jones College Powderpuff Team (2007-2011)
- Leadership Rice Mentorship Experience (Summer 2009)
- Pre-Law Undergraduate Scholars (Summer 2008)

CERTIFICATIONS & SKILLS

(3)
- Certified teacher in Louisiana for grades 1-5 (2012-2015)
- Speak Intermediate French, write basic French, and speak basic Spanish

Sample 3.6

After

Edited resume of Stacy Stevens (more than 3 years experience).

7345 Yale Ave. Apt 2E   stacyastevens@wustl.edu
St. Louis, MO 63130   504-123-4567

Stacy A. Stevens

EDUCATION

① **Washington University School of Law**   St. Louis, Missouri
J.D. Candidate   May 2018

② <u>Honors and Activities</u>
- Recipient - Dean's Fellowship ($X tuition for three years, faculty mentor, research assistantship)
- Finalist - 1L Client Counseling Competition (one of 24 teams out of 72 participating)
- Member - Women's Law Caucus - Auction Committee Member (largest student-led fundraiser designated for 2L public interest summer stipend)
- Member - Public Service Advisory Board-Public Service Committee; Black Law Students Association; International Law Society

① **Rice University**   Houston, Texas
Bachelor of Arts in Sociology, magna cum laude (GPA: X.XX/4.00)   May 2011

② <u>Honors and Activities</u>
- Inductee - *Phi Beta Kappa*
- Recipient - QuestBridge Scholarship ($X tuition and living expenses for four years)
- President - The Impact Movement (Rice chapter of national org.) - collaborated with Asst. Dean for Students to plan initiatives, drafted proposals for organization funding, served as liaison between campus and national organization, spearheaded on-campus outreach, and coordinated logistics for national conference
- Community Service Chair - Black Students Association (elected position) - coordinated community events
- Member - Advocating Diversity Association - Event Committee Member - secured sponsorship from local businesses, obtained funding from student government, and allocated facilities for program use

PUBLIC SERVICE & NON-PROFIT EXPERIENCE

The World Race   Asia, Europe, Africa
Participant and Logistics Coordinator (appointed position)   September 2013-August 2014
Traveled to 11 countries in 11 months as part of missionary team; raised $15,500 in funds through presentations and letters to board members and individual investors; partnered with local organizations and ministries to combat human trafficking, teach English, feed and clothe orphans, clean townships, and restore buildings; coordinated transportation, lodging, and administration for 40+ people; and served as liaison between on-site team and headquarters' logistics leader.

The Impact Movement   Orlando, FL
Assistant to Director of Communications   Summer 2010
Drafted promotional article for *The Orlando Times* to publicize organization; coordinated regular publishing opportunities for organization; redesigned marketing strategies; and developed conference materials for 1500 attendees.

LEGALLY RELATED EXPERIENCE

U. S. Equal Employment Opportunity Commission   Houston, TX
Legal Intern/Mentee   Summer 2009
Conducted research on case facts and witness history; reviewed legal memos and briefs for accuracy; attended witness deposition; shadowed director of district office; designed applicant database of over 300 contacts; and located witnesses.

TEACHING EXPERIENCE

Teach for America - Jackson Elementary School   Jackson, LA
Second Grade Teacher   July 2011-July 2013
Developed over 20 lessons and activities per week; facilitated student growth of 1.8 years in reading; managed 17 students in behavior and character development; created specialized plan for student needs; forged critical parent and student relationships in furtherance of common goal; and campaigned for county-wide tax initiative to benefit students.

St. Charles Parish Schools   Destrehan, LA
Substitute Teacher   August 2014-May 2015
Assisted special education students in schoolwork and recreation activities; completed individualized student plans and tracking charts; and coordinated with parents to implement student-specific goals.

SKILLS & INTERESTS

Languages: French (Limited Working Proficiency) and Spanish (Elementary Proficiency)
Alto - Gospel Choir

Notes:

1. Stacy added her law school. She included the date of her expected graduation and the date of her degree from her undergraduate school. She deleted her study abroad from her law school resume, since she has work experience that better highlights her international experience.

2. Stacy listed her honors and activities under each school and focused on her role as a "Recipient," "Inductee," or officer, as appropriate. Her listing of activities starts with the "best" or most relevant for her professional goals. Her Latin Honors are listed appropriately in italics right after her degree. Stacy included explanations of honors and activities as needed.

Checklist: Education

Schools Attended:	Yes	No
Did you identify every college or university that you attended using the institution's full name?		
Did you include the city, state, and, if appropriate, the country of each school?		
Did you include the date of graduation or the dates of attendance?		
If you attended a school outside the U.S., did you include the "Global University Ranking" published by *U.S. News & World Report*?		
Degrees:		
Did you specify the degree you received at each school?		
If you received more than one degree from a school, did you list each degree separately?		
If your school had majors and minors, did you include those?		
Latin Honors:		
If you graduated with Latin honors (*cum laude, magna cum laude,* or *summa cum laude*), did you include that in italics after your degree?		
Grades:		
Did you include your GPA for your majors and minors, if helpful, as well as your overall GPA for your undergraduate degree?		
If you included your GPA for your undergraduate and graduate degree, did you include it for your law school coursework?		
When you stated your GPA for your law school coursework, did you include individual grades for courses in which you excelled?		
If your legal research and writing grade was strong, did you include that separately from your overall GPA?		
If your law school or other school does not use a 4.0 scale, did you include an explanation of your GPA or individual course grade (i.e., top 10%)?		
If you attended a school outside the U.S. and your school does not use a 4.0 scale, did you convert your GPA to a 4.0 scale using a grade conversion calculator?		
If you attended a school outside the U.S. and you did not use a grade conversion calculator, did you include an explanatory note indicating the relative strength of your grade?		
Significant Writing and Publications:		
If you wrote a thesis prior to law school, did you include the title of the thesis, if appropriate for a legal resume?		
If your writing was published, did you include that publication using proper citation format provided by the publisher or, if not, using proper Bluebook form?		

Licenses, Certifications, and Visas:	Yes	No
Did you include relevant licenses, such as a CPA or Series 79, including the date you obtained it?		
If you are an international student studying in the U.S. under a student visa, did you include the type of visa and whether or not you have a work visa?		
Honors:		
Did you include scholarships you received both in undergraduate and law school, including an explanatory phrase identifying the amount or percentage of tuition covered by the scholarship?		
When you listed your scholarship, did you start the line with the word "Recipient" to keep the focus on you?		
If you are a member of an honor society, like *Phi Beta Kappa*, did you include the name and explanation of that society, if the name is not well known?		
When you listed your memberships, did you start with the word "Inductee" to keep the focus on you?		
If you graduated with departmental honors, did you include an explanation of those honors (i.e., top 10%)?		
Did you include other honors you received, such as Dean's List or book awards?		
Activities:		
Did you include activities in which you had an active or leadership role?		
Did you note whether or not you were elected or competitively selected for such activity?		
Did you begin your description using a word to describe your role, such as "Elected Representative" or "Treasurer"?		
Did you include activities that show a connection to a field or legal practice area?		
Did you answer the questions: "Why am I including this activity?" or "How does this activity relate to potential work with an Employer?" before including the activity?		
Proofing:		
Is the font consistent with the rest of your resume?		
Is this section formatted consistently with the rest of your resume?		
Are there any proofing errors (misspelled words, incorrect punctuation, etc.)?		

Chapter 4

Work Experience — General Information and Format: What Skill Categories Best Describe Your Work Experience?

As you know from Chapter 3, the top two qualities that an Employer looks for in law students are: 1) intelligence; and 2) professional skills. The next two chapters address the second quality. Your work experience, whether volunteer or for pay, is so important in highlighting your skills and abilities that I need two chapters to tell you the best way to convey it in your resume. Chapter 4 discusses how to structure the "Work Experience" section: its *format*. Chapter 5 addresses how to convey the specifics of your work experiences: the *substance* of what you actually did.

Purpose of Section

The purpose of this section of your resume is to organize your work experiences into meaningful categories so that an Employer can immediately see the relevance of your skills to their practice. To make this easier for them, choose resonant terms for those categories. Determining category terms is similar to finding "factors" in legal analysis; as you learned in law school, factors help attorneys figure out what courts consider in making a decision or a ruling. Use the same process with your work experience. Evaluate it and determine what factors, or categories, certain experiences have in common. This helps an Employer make a decision to interview and hire you.

Organizing your work experience into categories may not be something you have done before. Most students list their work experience in reverse chronological order, and use one heading: "Work Experience." For a law student — and most professionals — this is not that helpful. While a chronological organization may show a trajectory in career growth, it is more beneficial to show that trajectory within each work experience. So, let's talk about how you would choose category terms to describe your work experience by looking at some potential categories.

Step-by-Step Guide

First, review the work experiences listed on your pre-law school resume and determine what exactly you did in each job. Briefly identify the tasks you performed in order to determine which category best describes them. Second, begin grouping these tasks into no more than three categories. In law, three is a very common number (I don't know why) and Employers will be accustomed to this structure. Finally, list your categories in the order that would be most relevant to an Employer. As always, "Best goes first." If you are interested in working with a private law organization, for instance, start with categories that relate to for-profit business. If, however, you want to work for a public interest organization, begin with categories related to non-profit work.

As I mentioned in Chapter 3, you might even move some of the activities you included in the "Education" section to "Work Experience" if your role in those activities was significant. Doing so can be helpful if you do not have a lot of work experience between undergraduate and law school.

Typical Categories of Experiences

Legally Related Experience

Unless you have practiced law — and if you are in law school, you have not — you will not use the term "Legal Experience," as that is not truthful. One type of experience you might include in the "Legally Related Experience" category is employment with a traditional legal entity, such as a paralegal position. In addition, you may have interned with a judge or a legal public interest organization. Another example would be if you had a significant role in an honor council at one of your academic institutions.

Business Experience

If you have sales or marketing experience, that fits in this category. Sales and marketing experience is critical to legal organizations, which sell to clients the ability to get the job done efficiently and effectively. If you worked for a real estate company or bank, that experience also belongs in this category.

Teaching Experience

If you taught, tutored, or were a teaching assistant, that experience would be described here. Teaching experience directly relates to lawyering, which explains and interprets the law to clients, other attorneys, and judges.

Research Experience

Your research experience, even if it was not on a legally-related topic, is important, as it signals to an Employer that you know how to find information — a task attorneys perform every day. If you were a research assistant for a professor, include that information in this section. If your work led to a publication, include that here if it is not already listed under "Education."

Administrative Experience

The term "administrative experience" may bring to mind office-related tasks such as bookkeeping, filing, and answering phones. The kind of tasks you want to emphasize, however, are those in which you were in charge of projects or people. Experience in this category indicates that you have the professional skill of working with others: people whom you supervise and people who supervise you. In a legal environment, you will work with everyone — supervisee and supervisor — so experience in this area is a plus.

Leadership Experience

Many students overlook this type of experience. That is a mistake, as legal organizations look for law students whom they can see will eventually be in charge. Leadership experience is one in which you had more than a membership role, most likely one that you gained through a competitive selection process. Examples would be if you held a position of responsibility in a fraternity or sorority, or a leadership role in a school or community organization. You also gain leadership experience when in charge of a particular event, such as a conference, meeting, or fundraiser.

Professional Experience

This is a general term for experiences that are hard to categorize. It also works when you do not have a lot of work experience. In the latter case, it makes sense to put your experience in this one category and in reverse chronological order. While generally using two or three categories is most effective, if that does not work in your situation, "Professional Experience" is more persuasive than "Work Experience."

Selected Professional Experience

Many law students have a significant amount of experience and it would be challenging to include it all without their resume becoming unwieldy or difficult to read. In these cases, adding the term "Selected" before a particular category — like "Selected Professional Experience" or "Selected Business Experience" — works well. This indicates that you have additional experience but are only including what is most relevant.

Legally Related and Business Experience

Some students find it hard to separate the experiences they gained in a work environment. In that case, combining category terms works well. If you do combine terms, the two terms should be related to skills that Employers value.

Additional Tips for International Students

If you worked in a country other than the U.S., your job title might not be familiar to an Employer. Additionally, the title of your previous work experience may not accurately reflect all of the skills you used to do that work. For this section of your resume, you will want to think beyond job titles and more about the skills required to do that job. Use them to develop skill categories for your resume.

Chapter 4

Sample Resumes

Work Experience — General Information and Format

Sample 4.1

Before

Resume of Denise Hollander (0–1 year experience).

Notes:

1. Denise uses one category — "Experience" — to describe her work experience prior to law school. She includes that experience in reverse chronological order. This category and organization does not assist an Employer in understanding her skill set.

DENISE ALYSSA HOLLANDER
1234 West Pine Blvd #10L ● St. Louis, MO 63108
denisehollander@yahoo.com
(941) 123-4567

EDUCATION

University of South Florida   GPA: X.X
B.A., Summa Cum Laude - Mass Communications: December 2014
Concentration: Magazine Journalism
King O'Neal Scholar

❶ EXPERIENCE

Administrative Assistant, Oct. 2010-May 2015
Law Office of Theodore A. Gollnick, P.A.

Campus Fellow, Aug. 2013-May 2014
Committee for Accuracy in Middle East Reporting in America (CAMERA)
- Wrote op-eds and letters-to-the-editor for campus and local news outlets
- Organized educational events on campus

Vice President, Aug. 2013-May 2014
USF Hillel

Media Fellow, Summer 2013
The Israel Project, Washington, D.C.
- Wrote and revised weekly 2,000-word articles and received detailed individual feedback
- Wrote daily blog posts on current events in Israel and the Middle East
- Worked with key staff members through rotations in the Press, Social Media, and Research divisions
- Participated in weekly idea flow seminars with journalists, experts, and policymakers

Undergraduate Research Assistant, Aug. 2012-May 2013
USF Holocaust & Genocide Studies/Special & Digital Collections

MEMBERSHIPS & ACTIVITIES

Member, Phi Alpha Delta Legal Fraternity, Fall 2015-present
1L Representative, Jewish Law Society, Fall 2015-present
Kennel Enrichment Volunteer, Humane Society of Missouri, July 2015-present
CAMERA Annual Leadership and Advocacy Training Mission to Israel, June 2014
Jewish National Fund Alternative Spring Break in Israel, March 2014
Campus Liaison and Session Leader, Future Leaders for Israel Conference, March 2014
Student delegate, AIPAC Saban Leadership Conference, July 2013
Student delegate, Future Leaders for Israel Conference, April 2013
Student delegate, AIPAC Policy Conference, March 2013
Member, Sinai Scholars Society, USF Chabad, Spring 2012-present
Member, USF Pre-Law Society, Public Relations Committee, Fall 2012-Spring 2013

ACADEMIC AWARDS & HONORS

Top Scholar Award, Kappa Tau Alpha (National Journalism Honor Society), Fall 2014
Outstanding Volunteer Award, Hillels of the Florida Suncoast, Fall 2014
John & Jerry Wing Alexander Endowed Scholarship, USF Mass Communications, Fall 2014
Florida Medallion Scholarship, Fall 2011-Fall 2014
USF Director's Award, Fall 2011-Fall 2014
USF Tampa Campus Library Scholarship, Fall 2012-Spring 2013
Activist of the Year Award, AIPAC Policy Conference, March 2013
Bullitzer Prize, USF First Year Composition Program, Fall 2011

Sample 4.2

After

Edited resume of Denise Hollander (0–1 year experience).

DENISE ALYSSA HOLLANDER
1234 West Pine Blvd #10L • St. Louis, MO 63108
dahollander@wustl.edu
(941) 123-4567

EDUCATION

Washington University School of Law	**St. Louis**
J.D. Candidate	**May 2018**

Honors & Activities
Recipient: Dean's Fellowship Award (top 1L honor providing faculty and alumna mentor and research assistantship)
Recipient: The Cyrus P. & Jennie Austin Endowed Memorial Scholar in Law Award ($X tuition scholarship)
Appointed 1L Representative: Jewish Law Society
1L Representative: LearnLeo (online platform providing case-briefing and outlining tools for students)
Member: Phi Alpha Delta Legal Fraternity

University of South Florida	**Tampa**
B.A. in Mass Communications, *summa cum laude*	**Dec. 2014**

Concentration: Magazine Journalism
Selected Honors
Recipient: King O'Neal Scholar Award (awarded based on X.X GPA)
Recipient: Top Scholar Award, Kappa Tau Alpha (National Journalism Honor Society)
Recipient: John & Jerry Wing Alexander Endowed Scholarship, USF Mass Communications
Recipient: Bullitzer Prize, USF First Year Composition Program

❶ LEGALLY RELATED EXPERIENCE

Law Office of Theodore A. Gollnick, P.A., *Legal Intern*	**Sarasota**
	2010-2015
	Part time

- Drafted Proof of Service of Annual Guardianship Reports and proposed Orders
- E-filed Annual Guardianship Reports
- Obtained certified orders from Clerk's Office
- Conducted online court record and docket searches
- Drafted Petitions for Orders Authorizing Fees and Expenses

❷ RESEARCH & WRITING EXPERIENCE

The Israel Project, *Media Fellow*	**Washington, D.C.**
	Summer 2013

- Drafted weekly 2,000-word articles and revised same based on mentor's feedback
- Researched current events in Israel & Middle East and drafted daily blog posts
- Worked with key staff members through rotations in Press, Social Media, and Research divisions
- Participated in weekly idea flow seminars with journalists, experts, and policymakers
- Publication: *Israel's Acts of Charity Prove it is a Righteous Nation,* Algemeiner, Sept. 25, 2013

Committee for Accuracy in Middle East Reporting in America, *Campus Fellow*	**Tampa**
	2013-2014

- Drafted op-eds and letters-to-the-editor for campus and local news outlets
- Organized educational events on University of South Florida campus
- Participant: CAMERA Annual Leadership and Advocacy Training Mission to Israel

USF Holocaust & Genocide Studies/Special & Digital Collections, *Research Assistant*	**Tampa**
	2012-2013

❸ SELECTED LEADERSHIP EXPERIENCE

Elected Vice President: USF Hillel (Recipient: Outstanding Volunteer Award)	**2013-2014**
Recipient: Activist of the Year Award, AIPAC Policy Conference	**2013**
Campus Liaison & Session Leader: Future Leaders for Israel Conference	**2014**

COMMUNITY ENGAGEMENT

Jewish National Fund Alternative Spring Break in Israel	**2014**
Kennel Enrichment Volunteer: Humane Society of Missouri	**2015**

Notes:

1. The first skill category, "Legally Related Experience," is directly relevant to the legal internships Denise is seeking.

---

2. The second skill category, "Research and Writing Experience," showcases Denise's experience and skills in these areas, both of which are critical for an attorney's success.

---

3. The third category, "Selected Leadership Experience," includes Denise's experiences as an undergraduate. Because she does not have a lot of work experience between college and law school, she used this category to highlight her skills as a leader.

Sample 4.3

Before

Resume of Timothy Newstead (2–3 years experience).

Notes:

1. Tim uses two skill categories to describe his work experience: "Experience" and "Service." Neither category identifies the specific skills that would be relevant to an Employer.

2. The second skills category, "Service," is particularly confusing, as the word has several different connotations. A more specific term would convey information more quickly and accurately to an Employer.

Timothy J. Newstead

7424 Buckingham Dr., Apt. 2D, St. Louis, MO 63105 ~ (314) 123-4567 ~ newsteadt@wustl.edu

EDUCATION

Washington University in St. Louis School of Law	St. Louis, MO
Juris Doctor Candidate	May 2018

Honors: Scholar In Law Merit-Based Scholarship: $XXXX/year
Activities: 1L Client Counseling and Interviewing Competition Participant;
           Public Service Advisory Board Member

University of Notre Dame	Notre Dame, IN
Bachelor of Science in Science Pre-Professional: GPA X.XX	May 2012

Honors: University of Notre Dame Dean's List (Fall 2009)
Activities: Interhall Football Participant; Bengal Bouts Boxing Club Member;
           Friends of the Orphans Club Member; Pre-Professional Society Member

Southern Methodist University	Dallas, TX
GPA: X.X/4.0	Fall 2008-Spring 2009

❶ EXPERIENCE

Elman Law Group, LLC	Chicago, IL
Law Clerk	2014 - 2015

· Personal Injury law firm in downtown Chicago specializing in car accident cases
· Prepared summaries for settled cases and drafted legal correspondence
· Communicated with clients regarding the status of their cases

Passionist Volunteers International – Jamaica	Mandeville, Jamaica
Volunteer; Orientation Leader	2012-2013; 2014

· Assisted teachers and principal at St. Theresa Basic School
· Mentored boys at St. John Bosco Boy's Home
· Invited by director of the program to assist in four-week-long orientation program
· Initiated new volunteers into way of life for PVIs in Jamaica
· Mentored outgoing volunteers with respect on how to cope with leaving after year of service

Washington University Medical School	St. Louis, MO
Intern	2011

· Designed a database using Microsoft Access to organize quality improvement data
· Shadowed anesthesiologists at St. Louis Children's Hospital
· Helped with orientation for 3rd year medical students and interns

❷ SERVICE

Memorial Hospital	South Bend, IN
Ambassador	2012

· Volunteered in the pediatric unit of the hospital
· Interacted with patients and their families
· Worked with Child Life Specialist and provided support for patients and families

Slice of Life Club at University of Notre Dame	South Bend, IN
Volunteer Tutor	2011 - 2012

· Tutored children from ages five to 13 in math and reading
· Provided encouragement and support for children
· Developed a positive relationship with the children and serve as a mentor

SKILLS & INTERESTS

Language: Conversational in French
Interests: Notre Dame football, reading and writing, running

Sample 4.4

After

Edited resume of Timothy Newstead (2–3 years experience).

Timothy J. Newstead
7424 Buckingham Dr., Apt. 2D, St. Louis, MO 63105 ~ (314) 123-4567 ~ newsteadt@wustl.edu

EDUCATION

Washington University in St. Louis School of Law	St. Louis, MO
Juris Doctor Candidate	May 2018

Honors: Recipient - Scholar in Law Merit-Based Scholarship ($X/year for 3 years)
Activities: Participant - 1L Client Counseling and Interviewing Competition
Member - Public Service Advisory Board and Public Service Committee

University of Notre Dame	Notre Dame, IN
Bachelor of Science in Science Pre-Professional: GPA X.XX	May 2012

Honors: University of Notre Dame Dean's List (Fall 2009)
Activities: Member - Friends of the Orphans Club (public service organization); Participant - Interhall Football (full pad, tackle football – safety and kicker); Member - Bengal Bouts Boxing Club; Member - Pre-Professional Society

Southern Methodist University	Dallas, TX
GPA: X.X/4.0	Fall 2008-Spring 2009

❶ LEGALLY RELATED EXPERIENCE

Elman Law Group, LLC (Boutique Personal Injury Law Firm)	Chicago, IL
Law Clerk	2014-2015

Researched Illinois lien law and state laws relating to estate law and real property. Negotiated liens on behalf of clients with lien holders, including health care providers and insurance companies. Drafted motions to adjudicate liens and filed motions with Circuit Court. Drafted correspondence and communicated via telephone with clients regarding status of cases, including updates on settlement negotiations, court dates and depositions. Drafted letters to referring attorneys noting status of cases.

❷ TEACHING AND RESEARCH EXPERIENCE

Passionist Volunteers International – Jamaica	Mandeville, Jamaica
Orientation Leader, Teacher, Soccer Coach	2012-2013; 2014

Taught group of 5-year-old students with learning challenges in reading, writing, and math. Mentored boys at St. John Bosco Boy's Home, group home for at-risk youth, and coached Under 18 soccer team. Led retreats for Jamaican youth at St. Paul Catholic Retreat House. Invited by program director to assist in four-week-long orientation program. Initiated new volunteers into way of life for PVIs in Jamaica. Mentored outgoing volunteers on coping with leaving after service year.

Washington University Medical School (Anesthesiology Department at St. Louis Children's Hospital)	St. Louis, MO
Intern	2011

Designed database using Microsoft Access to organize quality improvement data. Data provided doctors with feedback from patients regarding patient care. Shadowed anesthesiologists at St. Louis Children's Hospital. Helped with orientation for M3 students and interns. Assisted orientation director with set-up for mock patient room which presented students with scenarios on how to deal with patient emergencies.

❸ COMMUNITY ENGAGEMENT

Memorial Hospital	South Bend, IN
Ambassador	2012

Volunteered in pediatric unit of hospital. Worked with Child Life Specialist and provided support for patients and families.

Slice of Life Club at University of Notre Dame	South Bend, IN
Tutor	2011-2012

Tutored children ages 5-13 in math and reading. Developed positive relationships with children and served as mentor.

SKILLS & INTERESTS

Language: Working proficiency in French
Interests: Notre Dame football, golf, reading (John Le Carré, Dennis Lehane, Alan Furst, Ken Follett), and writing (blog about College Football and wrote two screenplays at Notre Dame)

Notes:

1. Tim used three skill categories to describe his work experience. The first one, "Legally Related Experience," is easily understandable and directly relevant to a legal internship.

2. The second skill category, "Teaching and Research Experience," identifies two skills important to an Employer. Attorneys are always conducting legal research and "teaching" clients and other attorneys about the law.

3. Tim used the third skill category, "Community Engagement," to describe his volunteer experience. Attorneys are expected to volunteer in their communities, so this experience is important to Employers.

Sample 4.5

Before

Resume of Stacy Stevens (more than 3 years experience).

Notes:

1. Stacy uses only one skill category, "Experience," to describe her skills. Because she has several years of work experience between undergraduate and law school, it would be beneficial for her to more precisely delineate her skill set. She has listed her experience in reverse chronological order, which may not be helpful, depending on the type of legal internship she is seeking.

---

123 SMITHTON ST. • LAPLACE, LA 70068
STACYSTEVENS@YAHOO.COM • 123-4567 (CELL)

STACY STEVENS

EDUCATION & HONORS

Rice University, Houston, TX	August 2007-May 2011

Bachelor of Arts in Sociology awarded on: May 14, 2011 (GPA: X.XX/4.00)
- **Magna Cum Laude**
- **Phi Beta Kappa**
- President's Honor Roll: *Maintained a GPA that was in the top 30% of undergraduates*
- Leadership Rice Summer Mentorship Experience Fellow
- Pre-Law Undergraduate Scholars (PLUS) Outstanding Student at UNL-Law Program

University of Paris IV- Sorbonne, Paris, France	Spring 2010

Completed a study abroad program that focused on French language, history, and culture

❶ EXPERIENCE

The World Race	**Asia, Europe, Africa**
Logistics Coordinator	September 2013-August 2014

- Traveled to 11 countries in the span of 11 months as part of a missionary team
- Partnered with local organizations and ministries to serve the community and address social issues
- Led efforts to teach English, clean dumpsites, host children's camps, restore buildings, and distribute food
- Coordinated transportation, lodging, and administration for 40+ people

Jackson Elementary School	**Jackson, LA**
*Second Grade Teacher with **Teach for America***	July 2011-July 2013

- Developed over 20 lessons and activities per week, created resources, presented content on various topics
- Facilitated student growth of over 1.8 years in reading
- Managed 17 students in behavior and character development and addressed special needs a on case-by-case basis

Rice University Faculty Club	**Houston, TX**
Banquet Server/Waitress	January 2008-May 2011

- Facilitated satisfaction of over 150 customers through fulfillment of orders and resolution of complaints
- Improved atmosphere of facilities and maintained order of resources and supplies

The Impact Movement	**Orlando, FL**
Assistant to Director of Communications	Summer 2010

- Published a promotional article in two newspapers and forged a partnership between two organizations
- Redesigned marketing strategies and produced conference material for over 1500 attendees

U. S. Equal Employment Opportunity Commission	**Houston, TX**
Legal Intern/Mentee	Summer 2009

- Designed a large applicant database of over 300 contacts and located possible witnesses
- Conducted research on case facts and witness history and analyzed legal writings for accuracy
- Shadowed the lead attorney for his leadership abilities and completed leadership profiles of managers

ACTIVITIES

- Impact Movement, Conference Planner (2011-2012)
- Impact Movement, President (2007-2011)
- Black Student Union, Service Chair (2007-2011)
- Professional Development Advisor (2009-2011)
- Advocating Diversity Association (2008-2011)
- Melodious Voices Gospel Choir (2007-2011)
- Jones College Powderpuff Team (2007-2011)
- Leadership Rice Mentorship Experience (Summer 2009)
- Pre-Law Undergraduate Scholars (Summer 2008)

CERTIFICATIONS & SKILLS

- Certified teacher in Louisiana for grades 1-5 (2012-2015)
- Speak Intermediate French, write basic French, and speak basic Spanish

After

Edited resume of Stacy Stevens (more than 3 years experience).

7345 Yale Ave. Apt 2E
St. Louis, MO 63130

stacyastevens@wustl.edu
504-123-4567

Stacy A. Stevens

EDUCATION

Washington University School of Law — St. Louis, Missouri
J.D. Candidate — May 2018
Honors and Activities
- Recipient - Dean's Fellowship ($X tuition for three years, faculty mentor, research assistantship)
- Finalist - 1L Client Counseling Competition (one of 24 teams out of 72 participating)
- Member - Women's Law Caucus - Auction Committee Member (largest student-led fundraiser designated for 2L public interest summer stipend)
- Member - Public Service Advisory Board-Public Service Committee; Black Law Students Association; International Law Society

Rice University — Houston, Texas
Bachelor of Arts in Sociology, magna cum laude (GPA: X.XX/4.00) — May 2011
Honors and Activities
- Inductee - *Phi Beta Kappa*
- Recipient - QuestBridge Scholarship ($X tuition and living expenses for four years)
- President - The Impact Movement (Rice chapter of national org.) - collaborated with Asst. Dean for Students to plan initiatives, drafted proposals for organization funding, served as liaison between campus and national organization, spearheaded on-campus outreach, and coordinated logistics for national conference
- Community Service Chair - Black Students Association (elected position) - coordinated community events
- Member - Advocating Diversity Association - Event Committee Member - secured sponsorship from local businesses, obtained funding from student government, and allocated facilities for program use

❶ PUBLIC SERVICE & NON-PROFIT EXPERIENCE

The World Race — Asia, Europe, Africa
Participant and Logistics Coordinator (appointed position) — September 2013-August 2014
Traveled to 11 countries in 11 months as part of missionary team; raised $15,500 in funds through presentations and letters to board members and individual investors; partnered with local organizations and ministries to combat human trafficking, teach English, feed and clothe orphans, clean townships, and restore buildings; coordinated transportation, lodging, and administration for 40+ people; and served as liaison between on-site team and headquarters' logistics leader.

The Impact Movement — Orlando, FL
Assistant to Director of Communications — Summer 2010
Drafted promotional article for *The Orlando Times* to publicize organization; coordinated regular publishing opportunities for organization; redesigned marketing strategies; and developed conference materials for 1500 attendees.

❷ LEGALLY RELATED EXPERIENCE

U. S. Equal Employment Opportunity Commission — Houston, TX
Legal Intern/Mentee — Summer 2009
Conducted research on case facts and witness history; reviewed legal memos and briefs for accuracy; attended witness deposition; shadowed director of district office; designed applicant database of over 300 contacts; and located witnesses.

❸ TEACHING EXPERIENCE

Teach for America - Jackson Elementary School — Jackson, LA
Second Grade Teacher — July 2011-July 2013
Developed over 20 lessons and activities per week; facilitated student growth of 1.8 years in reading; managed 17 students in behavior and character development; created specialized plan for student needs; forged critical parent and student relationships in furtherance of common goal; and campaigned for county-wide tax initiative to benefit students.

St. Charles Parish Schools — Destrehan, LA
Substitute Teacher — August 2014-May 2015
Assisted special education students in schoolwork and recreation activities; completed individualized student plans and tracking charts; and coordinated with parents to implement student-specific goals.

SKILLS & INTERESTS
Languages: French (Limited Working Proficiency) and Spanish (Elementary Proficiency)
Alto - Gospel Choir

Notes:

1. Stacy used three skill categories to describe and accurately reflect her work experience. "Public Service & Non-Profit Experience" is an important category, as she is seeking a public interest legal internship.

2. "Legally Related Experience" describes her experience working in a government agency, which is directly relevant to the legal work she is seeking.

3. "Teaching Experience" reflects the years Stacy taught in public and private schools. Using these three categories to describe her skills gives an Employer important information about her experience and skill set.

Checklist: Work Experience — General Information and Format

Work Experience:	Yes	No
Have you identified the specific tasks or projects you did in each work experience prior to law school?		
Skill Categories:		
Have you identified a skill category that best describes the majority of tasks or projects for each work experience?		
If you do not have a lot of work experience between undergraduate and law school, are there some of your undergraduate activities that can be moved from the "Education" section of your resume to this section?		
Have you identified no more than three skill categories for use on your resume?		
Have you listed those three skill categories in order of the most relevant to an Employer regardless of chronology?		
Do you have experience in any of the following categories?		
Legally Related Experience?		
Business Experience?		
Teaching Experience?		
Research Experience?		
Administrative Experience?		
Leadership Experience?		
Professional Experience?		
Do you have too much experience to list on one page on your resume and therefore need to use the term "Selected" before your skill category?		
Proofing:		
Is the font for the skill category names consistent with the rest of your resume, although it may be slightly larger or in bold?		
Is this section formatted consistently with the rest of your resume?		
Are there any proofing errors (misspelled words, incorrect punctuation, etc.)?		

Chapter 5

Work Experience —
Substantive Descriptions:
What Specifically Did You Do
in Each Position You Held?

Purpose of Section

This section of your resume should describe your experience, paid and unpaid, in such a way that an Employer sees a clear connection between what you have done previously and what that Employer does today. This means that you will need to focus on tasks and accomplishments which reflect skills transferable to legal practice: effective written and oral communication; critical thinking; problem solving; working with a variety of people; efficient time management; leadership; and initiative. In this section, describe each work experience in terms that relate to one of the skill categories you identified in Chapter 4. You may end up tweaking those categories as you work your way through this chapter; sometimes when students identify the specific tasks and accomplishments within each work experience, they find that such experience fits better into another category than they originally thought.

Step-by-Step Guide

Previous Employer Name and Description

If your previous employer is well known, include the full name and, if commonly used, its acronym. For example, if you worked at the Environmental Protection Agency, you would include that term as well as the acronym (EPA), as most people refer to the agency by its acronym. Even if the previous employer's name is well known, you can still offer the additional information to show that you have knowledge relating to legal practice. For instance, if your previous employer is a publicly traded company, you can include the stock exchange symbol after its name; this indicates that you understand the difference between publicly traded and privately held companies, which is important for many legal practice areas, including securities regulation and corporate law. If your previous employer is not well known — for example, a smaller law firm or company that may not be known in your target geographic area — include a short description to explain the nature of the entity. Here are some examples:

CSI Leasing, Inc. (700+ employees and ~$19M in annual net income)
Note: ~ means approximately and M means million, terms business attorneys recognize

Tucker, Flyer and Lewis (boutique commercial transactional law firm — 45 attorneys)
Note: the term "boutique" is commonly used to describe law firms specializing in a particular legal practice area

Future Hope School (school for street children funded by HSBC)
Note: HSBC is the well-known acronym for the Hong Kong Shanghai Banking Corporation, which financial services attorneys will recognize

Regal Entertainment Group (NYSE: RGC)
Note: NYSE stands for New York Stock Exchange, a term corporate and securities attorneys recognize; RGC is the stock exchange symbol for the company

Job Title

If you had a specific job title, use it. If not, use typical legal terminology (e.g., Judicial or Legal Intern; Legal or Marketing Assistant; Research Assistant; Researcher) that fairly describes what you did. Until you graduate, refrain from using titles that are only appropriate for law graduates. For example, "Judicial Clerk" refers to a law school graduate who works with a judge in a formal clerkship program. A "Judicial Clerk" has very different responsibilities from a "Judicial Intern" and, therefore, the titles are not interchangeable. A job title like "Volunteer" is not persuasive, since it does not tell the Employer anything about what you did. Whether your position was paid is not relevant to whether you gained valuable experience.

Dates

Be consistent with dates on your entire resume. Use months and years or just years. If you describe the date of graduation in months and years, then do the same for your work experience. It doesn't matter whether you use numbers, the whole name of the month or an abbreviation, as long as you do so consistently. Many students hold positions for only a season, such as during the summer; if that is the case, you may decide to include the dates using that term and the years, especially if you have held the same position for more than one summer. As with the rest of your resume, be truthful. If you have worked somewhere for less than six months, do not use just the year. However, if you have worked somewhere for at least six months, it is truthful to use only the year. For consistency, if you included dates in the far right margin on the rest of your resume, do the same with these. (For examples, see the end of the chapter.)

Location

The location of your work experience offers another great opportunity to create a connection with an Employer. As in all legal writing, word choice matters; use it to your advantage. For example, if your geographic target area is Los Angeles and your previous employer was located in Santa Monica, you might want to use "Los Angeles" for the location, as this tells an Employer that you are willing to work in the broader geographic area. In contrast, if you are interested in working for a specific organization located in Brooklyn, you might want to use that term rather than "New York City."

Description of Tasks Accomplished and Responsibilities

You might need to rack your brain and research your work files to recall the specific projects you worked on and the skills they involved. This could take time, but it is critical to be very specific in this section of your resume, as an Employer will read it very carefully. Once you have a list of those specific projects, tasks, and responsibilities, order them according to our theme: "Best goes first." More complex tasks and projects that required greater responsibility and initiative belong at the top. Use specific descriptive terms, especially if those tasks and projects involved legally related matters. Action verbs keep the focus on you and your accomplishments. (A list of examples is included in Appendix E.) If you are no longer working at a position, use the past tense to describe your actions; if you are currently working, use the present tense.

Students often tell me that they don't have any legally related experience, but once they think back to what they did in a particular job, they discover that this is not true. For example, one former student of mine, David, had a job at a movie theater all through college and eventually worked his way up to manager. On his pre-law school resume, he'd used the following description for that job:

Regal Theater — Manager.
   Reconciled cash register, sent reports to home office, and ordered food service supplies.

I asked him a few questions, such as: Was the theater a local or national chain?; How large were your cash register receipts?; Did you reconcile those receipts daily, weekly, or monthly?; Did you draft the reports?; and Were you responsible for compliance with any federal or state regulations? He updated the description by adding specific details about the tasks and his responsibilities. Here is his revised version:

Regal Entertainment Group (NYSE: RGC).
   Manager — Regal Theater.
   Reconciled cash receipts of $20,000 daily. Drafted and submitted weekly reports regarding employee matters, income, and expenses to corporate headquarters. Responsible for compliance with Illinois Food Safety and Sanitation Act.

Same student, same job; but think about whom would you hire if you were an Employer. The second description shows a student who has experience with publicly traded corporations, financial transactions, drafting reports, and compliance with state regulations. As you can see, specific descriptions in terms that attorneys use can make a big difference in showing Employers that you have professional skills directly transferable to their practice.

Additional Tips for International Students

When including the name of your previous employer, if the entity is not internationally known, a short description is critical to helping an Employer understand the nature of your work experience. If your previous employer is a publicly traded company in a country other than the U.S., for example, include that company's stock exchange symbol or number and the specific stock exchange on which it is listed. For example, if you worked for LG Electronics in Korea, you would list the company as follows: LG Electronics Inc. KRX: 066570. When describing your tasks, accomplishments, and responsibilities, it is important to be very specific, since your job title may not accurately reflect all that you did at that employer in terms that a U.S. Employer would understand.

Chapter 5

Sample Resumes

Work Experience — Substantive Descriptions

Sample 5.1

Before

Resume of Denise Hollander (0–1 year experience).

Notes:

1. Listing the job title before the employer's name when that title is more administrative than substantive is not persuasive. The employer's practice and location is missing.

2. Denise uses the non-legal term "wrote" rather than the legal term "drafted."

3. This might be more effective if included under "Selected Leadership Experience."

4. Denise needs to include her published articles.

5. This would be more persuasive if listed under "Education."

DENISE ALYSSA HOLLANDER
1234 West Pine Blvd #10L ● St. Louis, MO 63108
denisehollander@yahoo.com
(941) 123-4567

EDUCATION

University of South Florida   GPA: X.X
B.A., Summa Cum Laude - Mass Communications: December 2014
Concentration: Magazine Journalism
King O'Neal Scholar

EXPERIENCE

① Administrative Assistant, Oct. 2010-May 2015
Law Office of Theodore A. Gollnick, P.A.

② Campus Fellow, Aug. 2013-May 2014
Committee for Accuracy in Middle East Reporting in America (CAMERA)
- Wrote op-eds and letters-to-the-editor for campus and local news outlets
- Organized educational events on campus

③ Vice President, Aug. 2013-May 2014
USF Hillel

④ Media Fellow, Summer 2013
The Israel Project, Washington, D.C.
- Wrote and revised weekly 2,000-word articles and received detailed individual feedback
- Wrote daily blog posts on current events in Israel and the Middle East
- Worked with key staff members through rotations in the Press, Social Media, and Research divisions
- Participated in weekly idea flow seminars with journalists, experts, and policymakers

⑤ Undergraduate Research Assistant, Aug. 2012-May 2013
USF Holocaust & Genocide Studies/Special & Digital Collections

MEMBERSHIPS & ACTIVITIES

Member, Phi Alpha Delta Legal Fraternity, Fall 2015-present
1L Representative, Jewish Law Society, Fall 2015-present
Kennel Enrichment Volunteer, Humane Society of Missouri, July 2015-present
CAMERA Annual Leadership and Advocacy Training Mission to Israel, June 2014
Jewish National Fund Alternative Spring Break in Israel, March 2014
Campus Liaison and Session Leader, Future Leaders for Israel Conference, March 2014
Student delegate, AIPAC Saban Leadership Conference, July 2013
Student delegate, Future Leaders for Israel Conference, April 2013
Student delegate, AIPAC Policy Conference, March 2013
Member, Sinai Scholars Society, USF Chabad, Spring 2012-present
Member, USF Pre-Law Society, Public Relations Committee, Fall 2012-Spring 2013

ACADEMIC AWARDS & HONORS

Top Scholar Award, Kappa Tau Alpha (National Journalism Honor Society), Fall 2014
Outstanding Volunteer Award, Hillels of the Florida Suncoast, Fall 2014
John & Jerry Wing Alexander Endowed Scholarship, USF Mass Communications, Fall 2014
Florida Medallion Scholarship, Fall 2011-Fall 2014
USF Director's Award, Fall 2011-Fall 2014
USF Tampa Campus Library Scholarship, Fall 2012-Spring 2013
Activist of the Year Award, AIPAC Policy Conference, March 2013
Bullitzer Prize, USF First Year Composition Program, Fall 2011

Sample 5.2

After

Edited resume of Denise Hollander (0–1 year experience).

DENISE ALYSSA HOLLANDER
1234 West Pine Blvd #10L • St. Louis, MO 63108
dahollander@wustl.edu
(941) 123-4567

EDUCATION

Washington University School of Law	**St. Louis**
J.D. Candidate	**May 2018**

Honors & Activities
Recipient: Dean's Fellowship Award (top 1L honor providing faculty and alumna mentor and research assistantship)
Recipient: The Cyrus P. & Jennie Austin Endowed Memorial Scholar in Law Award ($X tuition scholarship)
Appointed 1L Representative: Jewish Law Society
1L Representative: LearnLeo (online platform providing case-briefing and outlining tools for students)
Member: Phi Alpha Delta Legal Fraternity

University of South Florida	**Tampa**
B.A. in Mass Communications, *summa cum laude*	**Dec. 2014**

Concentration: Magazine Journalism
Selected Honors
Recipient: King O'Neal Scholar Award (awarded based on X.X GPA)
Recipient: Top Scholar Award, Kappa Tau Alpha (National Journalism Honor Society)
Recipient: John & Jerry Wing Alexander Endowed Scholarship, USF Mass Communications
Recipient: Bullitzer Prize, USF First Year Composition Program

LEGALLY RELATED EXPERIENCE

❶ **Law Office of Theodore A. Gollnick, P.A.**, *Legal Intern*	**Sarasota**	
• Drafted Proof of Service of Annual Guardianship Reports and proposed Orders	**2010-2015**	
• E-filed Annual Guardianship Reports	**Part time**	
• Obtained certified orders from Clerk's Office		
• Conducted online court record and docket searches		
• Drafted Petitions for Orders Authorizing Fees and Expenses		

RESEARCH & WRITING EXPERIENCE

❷ **The Israel Project**, *Media Fellow*	**Washington, D.C.**
• Drafted weekly 2,000-word articles and revised same based on mentor's feedback	**Summer 2013**
• Researched current events in Israel & Middle East and drafted daily blog posts	
• Worked with key staff members through rotations in Press, Social Media, and Research divisions	
• Participated in weekly idea flow seminars with journalists, experts, and policymakers	
• Publication: *Israel's Acts of Charity Prove it is a Righteous Nation*, Algemeiner, Sept. 25, 2013	
❸ **Committee for Accuracy in Middle East Reporting in America**, *Campus Fellow*	**Tampa**
• Drafted op-eds and letters-to-the-editor for campus and local news outlets	**2013-2014**
• Organized educational events on University of South Florida campus	
• Participant: CAMERA Annual Leadership and Advocacy Training Mission to Israel	
USF Holocaust & Genocide Studies/Special & Digital Collections, *Research Assistant*	**Tampa**
	2012-2013

SELECTED LEADERSHIP EXPERIENCE

❹ Elected Vice President: USF Hillel (Recipient: Outstanding Volunteer Award)	**2013-2014**
Recipient: Activist of the Year Award, AIPAC Policy Conference	**2013**
Campus Liaison & Session Leader: Future Leaders for Israel Conference	**2014**

COMMUNITY ENGAGEMENT

Jewish National Fund Alternative Spring Break in Israel	**2014**
Kennel Enrichment Volunteer: Humane Society of Missouri	**2015**

Notes:

1. Denise included the employer's location and a job title related to legal work she is seeking. Her task descriptions are very specific and use legal terminology. This shows that she has experience working with various legal documents.

---

2. This revised description is more specific and includes published articles. Including this work experience as "Research & Writing Experience" tells an Employer that she has skills critical to legal practice.

---

3. Denise used the legal term "drafted" rather than "wrote."

---

4. This makes more sense under the "Selected Leadership Experience."

Sample 5.3

Before

Resume of Timothy Newstead (2–3 years experience).

Notes:

1. Tim's task descriptions are somewhat generic and do not reflect all of his responsibilities at this firm.

2. "Volunteer" as a job title is not persuasive because it does not provide specific information about what Tim did in this position.

3. Tim's task descriptions are still too generic, especially the one describing his work with medical students and interns.

Timothy J. Newstead
7424 Buckingham Dr., Apt. 2D, St. Louis, MO 63105 ~ (314) 123-4567 ~ newsteadt@wustl.edu

EDUCATION

Washington University in St. Louis School of Law	St. Louis, MO
Juris Doctor Candidate	May 2018

Honors: Scholar In Law Merit-Based Scholarship: $XXXX/year
Activities: 1L Client Counseling and Interviewing Competition Participant; Public Service Advisory Board Member

University of Notre Dame	Notre Dame, IN
Bachelor of Science in Science Pre-Professional: GPA X.XX	May 2012

Honors: University of Notre Dame Dean's List (Fall 2009)
Activities: Interhall Football Participant; Bengal Bouts Boxing Club Member; Friends of the Orphans Club Member; Pre-Professional Society Member

Southern Methodist University	Dallas, TX
GPA: X.X/4.0	Fall 2008-Spring 2009

EXPERIENCE

❶ Elman Law Group, LLC — Chicago, IL — 2014 - 2015
Law Clerk
- Personal Injury law firm in downtown Chicago specializing in car accident cases
- Prepared summaries for settled cases and drafted legal correspondence
- Communicated with clients regarding the status of their cases

❷ Passionist Volunteers International – Jamaica — Mandeville, Jamaica — 2012-2013; 2014
Volunteer; Orientation Leader
- Assisted teachers and principal at St. Theresa Basic School
- Mentored boys at St. John Bosco Boy's Home
- Invited by director of the program to assist in four-week-long orientation program
- Initiated new volunteers into way of life for PVIs in Jamaica
- Mentored outgoing volunteers with respect on how to cope with leaving after year of service

❸ Washington University Medical School — St. Louis, MO — 2011
Intern
- Designed a database using Microsoft Access to organize quality improvement data
- Shadowed anesthesiologists at St. Louis Children's Hospital
- Helped with orientation for 3rd year medical students and interns

SERVICE

Memorial Hospital — South Bend, IN — 2012
Ambassador
- Volunteered in the pediatric unit of the hospital
- Interacted with patients and their families
- Worked with Child Life Specialist and provided support for patients and families

Slice of Life Club at University of Notre Dame — South Bend, IN — 2011 - 2012
Volunteer Tutor
- Tutored children from ages five to 13 in math and reading
- Provided encouragement and support for children
- Developed a positive relationship with the children and serve as a mentor

SKILLS & INTERESTS

Language: Conversational in French
Interests: Notre Dame football, reading and writing, running

After

Edited resume of Timothy Newstead (2–3 years experience).

Timothy J. Newstead

7424 Buckingham Dr., Apt. 2D, St. Louis, MO 63105 ~ (314) 123-4567 ~ newsteadt@wustl.edu

EDUCATION

Washington University in St. Louis School of Law	St. Louis, MO
Juris Doctor Candidate	May 2018

Honors: Recipient - Scholar in Law Merit-Based Scholarship ($X/year for 3 years)

Activities: Participant - 1L Client Counseling and Interviewing Competition
                 Member - Public Service Advisory Board and Public Service Committee

University of Notre Dame	Notre Dame, IN
Bachelor of Science in Science Pre-Professional: GPA X.XX	May 2012

Honors: University of Notre Dame Dean's List (Fall 2009)

Activities: Member - Friends of the Orphans Club (public service organization); Participant -
                 Interhall Football (full pad, tackle football – safety and kicker); Member - Bengal Bouts
                 Boxing Club; Member - Pre-Professional Society

Southern Methodist University	Dallas, TX
GPA: X.X/4.0	Fall 2008-Spring 2009

LEGALLY RELATED EXPERIENCE

❶ **Elman Law Group, LLC (Boutique Personal Injury Law Firm)**	Chicago, IL
Law Clerk	2014-2015

Researched Illinois lien law and state laws relating to estate law and real property. Negotiated liens on behalf of clients with lien holders, including health care providers and insurance companies. Drafted motions to adjudicate liens and filed motions with Circuit Court. Drafted correspondence and communicated via telephone with clients regarding status of cases, including updates on settlement negotiations, court dates and depositions. Drafted letters to referring attorneys noting status of cases.

TEACHING AND RESEARCH EXPERIENCE

❷ **Passionist Volunteers International – Jamaica**	Mandeville, Jamaica
Orientation Leader, Teacher, Soccer Coach	2012-2013; 2014

Taught group of 5-year-old students with learning challenges in reading, writing, and math. Mentored boys at St. John Bosco Boy's Home, group home for at-risk youth, and coached Under 18 soccer team. Led retreats for Jamaican youth at St. Paul Catholic Retreat House. Invited by program director to assist in four-week-long orientation program. Initiated new volunteers into way of life for PVIs in Jamaica. Mentored outgoing volunteers on coping with leaving after service year.

❸ **Washington University Medical School (Anesthesiology Department at St. Louis Children's Hospital)**	St. Louis, MO
Intern	2011

Designed database using Microsoft Access to organize quality improvement data. Data provided doctors with feedback from patients regarding patient care. Shadowed anesthesiologists at St. Louis Children's Hospital. Helped with orientation for M3 students and interns. Assisted orientation director with set-up for mock patient room which presented students with scenarios on how to deal with patient emergencies.

COMMUNITY ENGAGEMENT

Memorial Hospital	South Bend, IN
Ambassador	2012

Volunteered in pediatric unit of hospital. Worked with Child Life Specialist and provided support for patients and families.

Slice of Life Club at University of Notre Dame	South Bend, IN
Tutor	2011-2012

Tutored children ages 5-13 in math and reading. Developed positive relationships with children and served as mentor.

SKILLS & INTERESTS

Language: Working proficiency in French

Interests: Notre Dame football, golf, reading (John Le Carré, Dennis Lehane, Alan Furst, Ken Follett), and writing (blog about College Football and wrote two screenplays at Notre Dame)

Notes:

1. The description of the employer is helpful, as an Employer may not know this law firm. Tim used legal terms to describe the tasks he performed, which shows his familiarity with legal documents and proceedings.

---

2. Tim's description of his responsibilities is much more specific, and shows that he had more responsibility than is reflected in his "Before" description.

---

3. Tim's descriptions of this experience are more specific and include information about how the database was used, which would be interesting to an Employer.

Sample 5.5

Before

Resume of Stacy Stevens (more than 3 years experience).

Notes:

1. Stacy's description of this work experience is fairly general and does not reflect everything she did in this yearlong position.

2. The employer is a specific school that an Employer may not know. Leading with the sponsor of the program — Teach for America — would be more persuasive, as that organization is well known. The quantitative information included in the tasks description is impressive and persuasive.

3. The order of tasks and responsibilities is not persuasive, since it does not start with tasks involving a high level of responsibility or legally related tasks.

---

123 SMITHTON ST. • LAPLACE, LA 70068
STACYSTEVENS@YAHOO.COM • 123-4567 (CELL)
STACY STEVENS

EDUCATION & HONORS

Rice University, Houston, TX   August 2007-May 2011
Bachelor of Arts in Sociology awarded on: May 14, 2011 (GPA: X.XX/4.00)
- **Magna Cum Laude**
- **Phi Beta Kappa**
- President's Honor Roll: *Maintained a GPA that was in the top 30% of undergraduates*
- Leadership Rice Summer Mentorship Experience Fellow
- Pre-Law Undergraduate Scholars (PLUS) Outstanding Student at UNL-Law Program

University of Paris IV- Sorbonne, Paris, France   Spring 2010
Completed a study abroad program that focused on French language, history, and culture

EXPERIENCE

❶ The World Race   **Asia, Europe, Africa**
Logistics Coordinator   September 2013-August 2014
- Traveled to 11 countries in the span of 11 months as part of a missionary team
- Partnered with local organizations and ministries to serve the community and address social issues
- Led efforts to teach English, clean dumpsites, host children's camps, restore buildings, and distribute food
- Coordinated transportation, lodging, and administration for 40+ people

❷ Jackson Elementary School   **Jackson, LA**
Second Grade Teacher with **Teach for America**   July 2011-July 2013
- Developed over 20 lessons and activities per week, created resources, presented content on various topics
- Facilitated student growth of over 1.8 years in reading
- Managed 17 students in behavior and character development and addressed special needs a on case-by-case basis

Rice University Faculty Club   **Houston, TX**
Banquet Server/Waitress   January 2008-May 2011
- Facilitated satisfaction of over 150 customers through fulfillment of orders and resolution of complaints
- Improved atmosphere of facilities and maintained order of resources and supplies

The Impact Movement   **Orlando, FL**
Assistant to Director of Communications   Summer 2010
- Published a promotional article in two newspapers and forged a partnership between two organizations
- Redesigned marketing strategies and produced conference material for over 1500 attendees

U. S. Equal Employment Opportunity Commission   **Houston, TX**
Legal Intern/Mentee   Summer 2009
❸ - Designed a large applicant database of over 300 contacts and located possible witnesses
- Conducted research on case facts and witness history and analyzed legal writings for accuracy
- Shadowed the lead attorney for his leadership abilities and completed leadership profiles of managers

ACTIVITIES
- Impact Movement, Conference Planner (2011-2012)
- Impact Movement, President (2007-2011)
- Black Student Union, Service Chair (2007-2011)
- Professional Development Advisor (2009-2011)
- Advocating Diversity Association (2008-2011)
- Melodious Voices Gospel Choir (2007-2011)
- Jones College Powderpuff Team (2007-2011)
- Leadership Rice Mentorship Experience (Summer 2009)
- Pre-Law Undergraduate Scholars (Summer 2008)

CERTIFICATIONS & SKILLS
- Certified teacher in Louisiana for grades 1-5 (2012-2015)
- Speak Intermediate French, write basic French, and speak basic Spanish

Sample 5.6

After

Edited resume of Stacy Stevens (more than 3 years experience).

7345 Yale Ave. Apt 2E
St. Louis, MO 63130

stacyastevens@wustl.edu
504-123-4567

Stacy A. Stevens

EDUCATION

Washington University School of Law   St. Louis, Missouri
J.D. Candidate   May 2018
Honors and Activities
- Recipient - Dean's Fellowship ($X tuition for three years, faculty mentor, research assistantship)
- Finalist - 1L Client Counseling Competition (one of 24 teams out of 72 participating)
- Member - Women's Law Caucus - Auction Committee Member (largest student-led fundraiser designated for 2L public interest summer stipend)
- Member - Public Service Advisory Board-Public Service Committee; Black Law Students Association; International Law Society

Rice University   Houston, Texas
Bachelor of Arts in Sociology, magna cum laude (GPA: X.XX/4.00)   May 2011
Honors and Activities
- Inductee - *Phi Beta Kappa*
- Recipient - QuestBridge Scholarship ($X tuition and living expenses for four years)
- President - The Impact Movement (Rice chapter of national org.) - collaborated with Asst. Dean for Students to plan initiatives, drafted proposals for organization funding, served as liaison between campus and national organization, spearheaded on-campus outreach, and coordinated logistics for national conference
- Community Service Chair - Black Students Association (elected position) - coordinated community events
- Member - Advocating Diversity Association - Event Committee Member - secured sponsorship from local businesses, obtained funding from student government, and allocated facilities for program use

PUBLIC SERVICE & NON-PROFIT EXPERIENCE

 The World Race   Asia, Europe, Africa
Participant and Logistics Coordinator (appointed position)   September 2013-August 2014
Traveled to 11 countries in 11 months as part of missionary team; raised $15,500 in funds through presentations and letters to board members and individual investors; partnered with local organizations and ministries to combat human trafficking, teach English, feed and clothe orphans, clean townships, and restore buildings; coordinated transportation, lodging, and administration for 40+ people; and served as liaison between on-site team and headquarters' logistics leader.

The Impact Movement   Orlando, FL
Assistant to Director of Communications   Summer 2010
Drafted promotional article for *The Orlando Times* to publicize organization; coordinated regular publishing opportunities for organization; redesigned marketing strategies; and developed conference materials for 1500 attendees.

LEGALLY RELATED EXPERIENCE

 U. S. Equal Employment Opportunity Commission   Houston, TX
Legal Intern/Mentee   Summer 2009
Conducted research on case facts and witness history; reviewed legal memos and briefs for accuracy; attended witness deposition; shadowed director of district office; designed applicant database of over 300 contacts; and located witnesses.

TEACHING EXPERIENCE

 Teach for America - Jackson Elementary School   Jackson, LA
Second Grade Teacher   July 2011-July 2013
Developed over 20 lessons and activities per week; facilitated student growth of 1.8 years in reading; managed 17 students in behavior and character development; created specialized plan for student needs; forged critical parent and student relationships in furtherance of common goal; and campaigned for county-wide tax initiative to benefit students.

St. Charles Parish Schools   Destrehan, LA
Substitute Teacher   August 2014-May 2015
Assisted special education students in schoolwork and recreation activities; completed individualized student plans and tracking charts; and coordinated with parents to implement student-specific goals.

SKILLS & INTERESTS

Languages: French (Limited Working Proficiency) and Spanish (Elementary Proficiency)
Alto - Gospel Choir

Notes:

1. Stacy added the specific amount of funds she raised and how she raised them. She included her interactions with board members and investors — two groups of people she may work with as an attorney.

2. Stacy re-ordered the tasks she accomplished in order of greatest responsibility. Rather than "legal writings," she used the more sophisticated terms "legal memos and briefs."

3. Stacy added her work experience in the countywide tax initiative, which adds another skill to her skill set.

Checklist: Work Experience — Substantive Descriptions

Employer:	Yes	No
Did you include the employer's full name and, if applicable, commonly understood acronym?		
If the employer is a publicly traded company, did you include the stock exchange symbol for it?		
If the employer is a publicly traded company headquartered outside of the U.S., did you also include the applicable stock exchange?		
If the employer is not well known, did you include a description of it next to the name?		
Job Title:		
If you had a specific job title, did you use it?		
If not, did you use a title that fairly describes the job, using terminology commonly used in legal practice?		
Did you refrain from using the term "volunteer"?		
Dates:		
Did you state the dates for all of your work experience using consistent terms — either months and years or just years?		
If you used abbreviations for months, did you use them consistently?		
Location:		
Did you choose to use a specific or a general location based on your target area?		
Description of Tasks:		
Did you use specific terms to describe your tasks and responsibilities?		
Did you list the tasks and responsibilities consistent with "best goes first"?		
Did you use action verbs to keep the focus on you rather than the task or responsibility? (See Appendix E for a list of action verbs.)		
Did you use the past tense to describe a past work experience?		
Did you use the present tense to describe current or on going work experience?		
Proofing:		
Is the font consistent with the rest of your resume, although the name of the employer and job title may be in bold or italics?		
Is this section formatted consistently with the rest of your resume?		
Are there any proofing errors (misspelled words, incorrect punctuation, etc.)?		

Chapter 6

Special Skills and Interests: What Do You Do Outside of Law School and Work?

Purpose of Section

The "Special Skills and Interests" section of your resume tells Employers what makes you unique, to pique their interest in you. This section has the added bonus of providing Employers with things to talk about during the interview so they can avoid asking you to "tell us about yourself." As with the rest of your resume, be specific about your skills and interests. This will set you apart from other applicants.

Step-by-Step Guide

Special Skills

Languages

Many law students possess the ability to speak and read more than one language. If you are interested in any kind of international law field, speaking more than one language is probably required. When you describe your level of proficiency, be truthful. Assume that you and your interviewer could start conversing in that language during the interview. If you are including your language skills and do not plan to practice internationally, or an Employer does not need such skills for their practice, you can use general terms to describe your conversational, writing, and reading capabilities. Words such as "conversational" or "fluent" will be sufficient.

However, if your language skills are essential for your future legal practice or to an Employer, you will want to use much more specific terminology. In that instance, applying a well-known standard such as the Language Proficiency Definitions used by the U.S. Department of State would be best. This signals your sophistication regarding international standards; an Employer will be impressed that you are aware of them.

The current definitions are:

U.S. Department of State: Language Proficiency Definitions

Proficiency Code	Speaking Definitions	Reading Definitions
0 - No Practical Proficiency	No practical speaking proficiency.	No practical reading proficiency.
1 - Elementary Proficiency	Able to satisfy routine travel needs and minimum courtesy requirements.	Able to read some personal and place names, street signs, office and shop designations, numbers, and isolated words and phrases.
2 - Limited Working Proficiency	Able to satisfy routine social demands and limited work requirements.	Able to read simple prose, in a form equivalent to typescript or printing, on subjects within a familiar context.
3 - Minimum Professional Proficiency	Able to speak the language with sufficient structural accuracy and vocabulary to participate effectively in most formal and informal conversations on practical, social, and professional topics.	Able to read standard newspaper items addressed to the general reader, routine correspondence, reports, and technical materials in the individual's special field.
4 - Full Professional Proficiency	Able to use the language fluently and accurately on all levels pertinent to professional needs.	Able to read all styles and forms of the language pertinent to professional needs.
5 - Native or Bilingual Proficiency	Equivalent to that of an educated native speaker.	Equivalent to that of an educated native.

http://careers.state.gov/gateway/lang_prof_def.html

Additional Tips for International Students

It is not necessary to include English as one of the languages in which you are proficient if you plan to work in the U.S., as it will be assumed that you speak, read, and write English fluently if you are studying there. If, however, you are applying for legal internships outside of the U.S., it might be helpful to include your level of English fluency using the Department of State standards included above.

Computer Skills

Another special skill is the ability to use specialized computer programs. If you are interested in pursuing a career that requires them, include those in this section of your resume. For example, if you are interested in pursuing corporate legal work and know how to use sophisticated financial software, you'll want to indicate that knowledge here. In addition, if you have a certification in a specialized computer program that is relevant to your future legal practice or an Employer, include that certification in the "Education" section of your resume rather than "Special Skills and Interests." Remember, "Best goes first."

Proficiency with general computer programs, such as Excel, Word, Lexis, Westlaw, Bloomberg Law, or other legal research platforms does not count among your "special skills"; an Employer will expect that you possess this. Specialized computer software skills — such as expertise with publishing programs, unless necessary for your legal practice — also should not be included on your resume.

Interests

Because you will be working closely with others and Employers want to make sure you are a "good fit," they will want to know something about you personally. This is a great section to include interests that make you unique and that will pique an Employer's curiosity. However, do not include personal information that an Employer does not need to know, such as marital status. In addition, do not list generic interests such as "travel, cooking, or exercising" since those terms do not tell an Employer anything unique about you. However, if you can be more specific about one of those interests, then you do want to include that in this section. For example, if you "rode a bicycle across China" (yes, I had a student who did that), or are enthralled with "Cuban cooking," that is worth including, since this information creates an opportunity for an Employer to ask you questions. If you completed a marathon or participated in the "Wall Street Weightlifting" event, you could include that here, as well.

References

You may be wondering if you should include a statement that says something like "References Upon Request" or list references on your resume. Neither should be included for several reasons. First, if an Employer wants references, they will ask and you will provide them. Second, waiting to provide references gives you another opportunity to contact an Employer. The more chances you have to contact an Employer and stay "top-of-mind," the better. Third, if you have been following the guidelines in this book, your resume will be chock-full of interesting information, with no room to include references. Finally, just as your resume is a fluid document, an ever-developing story, so, too, are your references. You'll want to pick and choose references based on which provide the most relevant information about you given the nature of the job and the Employer. (Chapter 13 includes detailed information about obtaining references.)

Chapter 6

Sample Resumes

Special Skills and Interests

Sample 6.1

Before

Resume of Frank Douglas (0–1 year experience).

Notes:

1. The term "extracurricular activities" is used for undergraduate resumes and is not appropriate for a legal resume. Relevant activities should be included under the university in which Frank participated in them. Activities should be separated from interests.

2. Frank needs to add specifics to the interests to provide more detail.

3. Several languages are a real plus, but Frank needs to use commonly understood terms to describe his fluency.

Frank Douglas
18 Chase Ct., Lawrenceville, NJ 08648 • (609) 123-4567 • fd@columbia.edu

EDUCATION
The Lawrenceville School, Lawrenceville, NJ   September 2006 - June 2010
High School Diploma

Columbia University, New York, NY   September 2010 - May 2014
Bachelor of Arts - Economics-Philosophy
Coursework:
    <u>Economics</u>
    Globalization and its Risks
    Economic Organization and Development of China
    International Trade
    Urban Economics
    <u>Philosophy</u>
    Philosophical Problems of Climate Change
    Philosophy of Law
    Ethics
    <u>Other/Interdisciplinary</u>
    Economics-Philosophy Seminar (Seminar focusing on the economic, philosophic, and political issues surrounding climate change)
    Introduction to Film Theory
    The Social World
    The Rise of Civilization
    Introduction to Comparative Politics

WORK EXPERIENCE
American School in Japan, Tokyo, Japan   July 2009-August 2009
Camp Counselor

Columbia University, New York, NY   June 2011-August 2011
General Assistant   June 2012-August 2012
-Performed basic assistant work in IT Department of Butler Library

Institute for Advanced Study, Princeton, NJ   June 2013-August 2013
Public Affairs Intern   June 2014-August 2014
-Duties consisted mostly of fact-checking and copy editor

❶ EXTRACURRICULAR ACTIVITIES AND INTERESTS
Completed Leadership Training Course at YMCA Camp Mason, NJ, in July and August of 2008
Staff Writer for high school newspaper
Member of Young Democrats in high school
Member of Columbia Democrats in college
❷ Special Interests in Cinema, American literature, and Japanese culture and language

❸ LANGUAGES
Native speaker of English
Fluent in Italian and French
Reading knowledge of Spanish
Learning Japanese

After

Edited resume of Frank Douglas (0–1 year experience).

School Address:	**Frank D. Douglas**	Permanent Address:
1234 Lindell Blvd., Apt. W-504	(609) 123-4567	18 Chase Ct.
St. Louis, MO 63108	fddouglas@wustl.edu	Lawrenceville, NJ 08648

EDUCATION

Washington University School of Law   St. Louis, MO – 2018
J.D. Candidate
- Recipient - Scholar in Law Award ($X/year merit scholarship)
- Board Member - Energy and Environmental Law Society
- Member - International Law Society

Columbia University   New York, NY – 2014
B.A., Economics and Philosophy
- Dean's List - Fall 2013 & Spring 2014
- Op-Ed Writer - Columbia Spectator (school newspaper)
- Member - Columbia Democrats

PROFESSIONAL EXPERIENCE

Lutheran Social Ministries of New Jersey   Trenton, NJ – 2015
ESL Teacher
     Taught adult classes in English. Worked with groups of varying ability to improve their grammar and vocabulary. Assisted in developing lessons and evaluating student ability through written and verbal tests. Taught citizenship classes to students attempting to gain U.S. citizenship, with lessons in history and civics.

Institute for Advanced Study   Princeton, NJ – 2013-2014
Public Affairs Intern
     Reviewed and edited press releases. Updated website page on faculty publications and ran Excel functions to find anomalies in database cataloging term lengths of over 300 scholars. Collected biographical and autobiographical material on multiple faculty members. Drafted summaries of faculty members' life and work in preparation for retirement celebrations. Reviewed lists of scholars arriving from other institutions to make sure international institution names had been translated correctly.

Columbia University   New York, NY – 2011-2012
Information Technology General Assistant
     Assisted IT department in hardware repairs and software installations on staff computers. Contacted Dell and Hewlett-Packard for information on warranties and to order replacements for malfunctioning material still covered under warranty.

American School in Japan   Tokyo, Japan – 2009
Camp Counselor
     Responsible for group of 15 children aged 10-13. Assisted them in activities designed to aid them in learning English. Met with parents to discuss progress of children.

① SPECIAL INTERESTS
American literature (Hemingway especially) and film (Film Noir, French New Wave)
Fan of football and soccer (played both in high school)
② Member of Alumni Association of the Lawrenceville School, in NJ

③ LANGUAGES
Fluent in Italian and French
Reading knowledge of Spanish

Notes:

1. Frank added detail to describe his interests, including specific authors he enjoys reading and film genres he enjoys watching. He added his interests in sports and described his participation.

2. Frank added his membership in his well-known private high school alumni association as a way to include his connection to his target city. High schools no longer belong in the "Education" section of a legal resume.

3. Frank focused on the languages in which he is most competent, using easily understood terms to describe his fluency.

Sample 6.3

Before

Resume of Sally Nathan (2–3 years experience).

Notes:

1. Sally includes standard computer program skills that are not relevant to the legal jobs she is seeking. These should be deleted from her resume.

2. "References upon request" should not be included on a resume. See Chapter 13 for a discussion of how to provide references.

Sally Nathan

1234 Vine Street, Dallas, TX 75204 | (C) (314) 123-4567 snathan@yahoo.com

Professional Summary

High-energy, organized account manager with effective project and personnel management skills. Always willing to go the extra mile for on-time content delivery and customer satisfaction.

Education

The University of Kansas, School of Journalism   Lawrence, KS
Bachelor of Science, Journalism, Bachelor of Arts - GPA: X.XX   May
2013
KU Honor Roll Recipient (8 semesters)
Language, Literature and Culture Study Abroad Program   Barcelona, Spain
• Immersion into different cultures   Summer 2012
• Used communication and organization skills to navigate through new cities

Work History

ISNetworld Software Corporation   Dallas, TX
Senior Associate   July 2014 – Present
• Account manager for multiple clients in the Midstream and Pipelines industry
        • Kinder Morgan, Plains All American, TransCanada, Alliance Pipelines, Plains Midstream Canada, Williams
• Coordinate and target customer service assistance plans for clients throughout the United States and Canada
• Travel 20-50 percent for management meetings, networking events and prospecting
Customer Service Representative   August 2013- July 2014
• Learned to communicate effectively and handle escalated customer situations
• Worked with the branding team to research and publish customer case studies to the ISN website
• Learned to speak and convey information in front of large groups

Fuksa Khorshid, LLC   Chicago, IL
Legal Intern   June 2012 – August 2012
• Strengthened reading comprehension, gained in-depth research and analytical thinking skills
• Oversaw logistics and handled donor relations as a chair for a fundraiser event that raised more than $50,000 for Chicago charities
• Gained business and patent law exposure by attending depositions and client meetings

Volunteer/Collegiate Activities

OSHA Oil and Gas Conference   Houston, TX
Volunteer   December 2014
• Handled registration for more than 2,000 attendees, organized donated items in gift bags and assisted with attendee questions
Pi Beta Phi: Kansas Alpha Chapter Member   August 2009 – May 2013
Technology Chair
• Made sure all computers, printers, televisions and projectors were working properly on a daily basis
• Proactively replaced outdated software and established a relationship with outside vendors
Natural Ties Volunteer Program   August 2012 – May 2013
Member
• Interacted with mentally disabled seniors through a variety of weekly activities
University of Kansas Track and Field Team   July 2009 – July 2010
• *All Big 12 Athlete*

Honors/Awards

• Jayhawk Generations Scholarship, The University of Kansas (2009–2013) • National Society for Collegiate Scholars (2010–2013)
• Golden Key Honor Society (2011–2013) • Big 12 Indoor Track and Field Championships – Seventh Place (2010)

Skills

❶ • MS Office Suite • Microsoft Excel • Microsoft PowerPoint •In-house customer relationship management (CRM) platform
• Final Cut Pro • iMovie

❷ *References upon request

After

Edited resume of Sally Nathan (2–3 years experience).

Notes:

1. Sally deleted her skills and included specific interests that will provide an Employer with something to talk about with her in an interview.

Sally Nathan

123 Lake Drive　　　　　　　　　　　　　　　　　　　(314) 123-4567
Kirkwood, MO 63122　　　　　　　　　　　　　　　　snathan@wustl.edu

EDUCATION

Washington University School of Law　　　　　　　　St. Louis, MO
J.D. Candidate: May 2018
Honors and Activities:
　　Winner – 1L Client Competition (70 teams)
　　1L Elected Representative – Student Bar Association
　　1L Elected Representative – Phi Alpha Delta
　　Member – Wash U Out West (WOW)
　　Member – Sports and Entertainment Law Society

University of Kansas　　　　　　　　　　　　　　　Lawrence, KS
B.S., Journalism, May 2013 – GPA: X.XX
Honors and Activities:
　　Recruit - Heptathlete – D1 Track and Field
　　Medalist - All Big 12 Track and Field
　　Recipient - Jayhawk Generations Scholarship
　　Member - National Society for Collegiate Scholars
　　Member and Technology Chair – Pi Beta Phi

Sant Jordi University　　　　　　　　　　　　　　Barcelona, Spain
Language, Literature and Culture Study Abroad Program　　Summer 2013

LEGALLY RELATED AND BUSINESS EXPERIENCE

ISNetworld Software Corporation　　　　　　　　　　Dallas, TX
　Senior Associate　　　　　　　　　　　　　　　July 2014–June 2015
Reviewed OSHA documents (300A and 300log), workers' compensation claims, insurance documents (including general and employers' liability) and safety programs for regulatory compliance. Primary account manager for large clients in Oil and Gas Industry (Kinder Morgan, Plains All American, TransCanada, Alliance Pipelines, Plains Midstream Canada). Developed and presented programs to potential contractors (200-300 attendees) regarding clients' compliance requirements. Team lead during management meetings and prospective client meetings for senior management of Oil and Gas companies. Position involved extensive travel throughout the United States and Canada.
　Associate　　　　　　　　　　　　　　　　　August 2013–July 2014
Communicated and deescalated customer conflicts in person and via phone. Researched and drafted customer case studies for company website. Trained new employees on company protocols.

Fuksa Khorshid, LLC　　　　　　　　　　　　　　Chicago, IL
　Legal Intern　　　　　　　　　　　　　　　　June 2012–August 20
Assisted partner during depositions and client meetings. Appointed as co-chair for fundraiser event that raised more than $50,000 for Chicago Charities. Attended hearings in small claims court.

OTHER LEADERSHIP AND COMMUNITY ENGAGEMENT

OSHA Oil and Gas Conference　　　　　　　　　　Houston, TX
　Volunteer: December 2014
Responsible for registration of 2,000+ attendees. Interfaced/worked with OSHA and Oil and Gas representatives.

Natural Ties Volunteer Program　　　　　　　　　Lawrence, KS
　Volunteer: August 2009–May 2013
Interacted with mentally challenged seniors through variety of weekly activities.

❶ INTERESTS

Violinist, Equestrian (hunter/jumper), Runner (half marathons), Softball

Sample 6.5

Before

Resume of Stacy Stevens (more than 3 years experience).

Notes:

1. Teacher Certification should be included in "Experience" under the "Jackson Elementary School" entry, as it relates to that position. However, Stacy may not want to include the certification on her resume at all, as it was only valid for a limited time in one state and has expired.

2. Language skills are important but Stacy's fluency descriptions are unclear.

---

123 SMITHTON ST. • LAPLACE, LA 70068
STACYSTEVENS@YAHOO.COM • 123-4567 (CELL)
STACY STEVENS

EDUCATION & HONORS

Rice University, Houston, TX   August 2007-May 2011
Bachelor of Arts in Sociology awarded on: May 14, 2011 (GPA: X.XX/4.00)
- **Magna Cum Laude**
- **Phi Beta Kappa**
- President's Honor Roll: *Maintained a GPA that was in the top 30% of undergraduates*
- Leadership Rice Summer Mentorship Experience Fellow
- Pre-Law Undergraduate Scholars (PLUS) Outstanding Student at UNL-Law Program

University of Paris IV- Sorbonne, Paris, France   Spring 2010
Completed a study abroad program that focused on French language, history, and culture

EXPERIENCE

The World Race   **Asia, Europe, Africa**
Logistics Coordinator   September 2013-August 2014
- Traveled to 11 countries in the span of 11 months as part of a missionary team
- Partnered with local organizations and ministries to serve the community and address social issues
- Led efforts to teach English, clean dumpsites, host children's camps, restore buildings, and distribute food
- Coordinated transportation, lodging, and administration for 40+ people

Jackson Elementary School   **Jackson, LA**
*Second Grade Teacher with **Teach for America***   July 2011-July 2013
- Developed over 20 lessons and activities per week, created resources, presented content on various topics
- Facilitated student growth of over 1.8 years in reading
- Managed 17 students in behavior and character development and addressed special needs a on case-by-case basis

Rice University Faculty Club   **Houston, TX**
Banquet Server/Waitress   January 2008-May 2011
- Facilitated satisfaction of over 150 customers through fulfillment of orders and resolution of complaints
- Improved atmosphere of facilities and maintained order of resources and supplies

The Impact Movement   **Orlando, FL**
Assistant to Director of Communications   Summer 2010
- Published a promotional article in two newspapers and forged a partnership between two organizations
- Redesigned marketing strategies and produced conference material for over 1500 attendees

U. S. Equal Employment Opportunity Commission   **Houston, TX**
Legal Intern/Mentee   Summer 2009
- Designed a large applicant database of over 300 contacts and located possible witnesses
- Conducted research on case facts and witness history and analyzed legal writings for accuracy
- Shadowed the lead attorney for his leadership abilities and completed leadership profiles of managers

ACTIVITIES

- Impact Movement, Conference Planner (2011-2012)
- Impact Movement, President (2007-2011)
- Black Student Union, Service Chair (2007-2011)
- Professional Development Advisor (2009-2011)
- Advocating Diversity Association (2008-2011)
- Melodious Voices Gospel Choir (2007-2011)
- Jones College Powderpuff Team (2007-2011)
- Leadership Rice Mentorship Experience (Summer 2009)
- Pre-Law Undergraduate Scholars (Summer 2008)

CERTIFICATIONS & SKILLS

- **1** • Certified teacher in Louisiana for grades 1-5 (2012-2015)
- **2** • Speak Intermediate French, write basic French, and speak basic Spanish

Sample 6.6

After

Edited resume of Stacy Stevens (more than 3 years experience).

7345 Yale Ave. Apt 2E
St. Louis, MO 63130

stacyastevens@wustl.edu
504-123-4567

Stacy A. Stevens

EDUCATION

Washington University School of Law	St. Louis, Missouri
J.D. Candidate	May 2018

Honors and Activities
- Recipient - Dean's Fellowship ($X tuition for three years, faculty mentor, research assistantship)
- Finalist - 1L Client Counseling Competition (one of 24 teams out of 72 participating)
- Member - Women's Law Caucus - Auction Committee Member (largest student-led fundraiser designated for 2L public interest summer stipend)
- Member - Public Service Advisory Board-Public Service Committee; Black Law Students Association; International Law Society

Rice University	Houston, Texas
Bachelor of Arts in Sociology, magna cum laude (GPA: X.XX/4.00)	May 2011

Honors and Activities
- Inductee - *Phi Beta Kappa*
- Recipient - QuestBridge Scholarship ($X tuition and living expenses for four years)
- President - The Impact Movement (Rice chapter of national org.) - collaborated with Asst. Dean for Students to plan initiatives, drafted proposals for organization funding, served as liaison between campus and national organization, spearheaded on-campus outreach, and coordinated logistics for national conference
- Community Service Chair - Black Students Association (elected position) - coordinated community events
- Member - Advocating Diversity Association - Event Committee Member - secured sponsorship from local businesses, obtained funding from student government, and allocated facilities for program use

PUBLIC SERVICE & NON-PROFIT EXPERIENCE

The World Race	Asia, Europe, Africa
Participant and Logistics Coordinator (appointed position)	September 2013-August 2014

Traveled to 11 countries in 11 months as part of missionary team; raised $15,500 in funds through presentations and letters to board members and individual investors; partnered with local organizations and ministries to combat human trafficking, teach English, feed and clothe orphans, clean townships, and restore buildings; coordinated transportation, lodging, and administration for 40+ people; and served as liaison between on-site team and headquarters' logistics leader.

The Impact Movement	Orlando, FL
Assistant to Director of Communications	Summer 2010

Drafted promotional article for *The Orlando Times* to publicize organization; coordinated regular publishing opportunities for organization; redesigned marketing strategies; and developed conference materials for 1500 attendees.

LEGALLY RELATED EXPERIENCE

U. S. Equal Employment Opportunity Commission	Houston, TX
Legal Intern/Mentee	Summer 2009

Conducted research on case facts and witness history; reviewed legal memos and briefs for accuracy; attended witness deposition; shadowed director of district office; designed applicant database of over 300 contacts; and located witnesses.

TEACHING EXPERIENCE

Teach for America - Jackson Elementary School	Jackson, LA
Second Grade Teacher	July 2011-July 2013

Developed over 20 lessons and activities per week; facilitated student growth of 1.8 years in reading; managed 17 students in behavior and character development; created specialized plan for student needs; forged critical parent and student relationships in furtherance of common goal; and campaigned for county-wide tax initiative to benefit students.

St. Charles Parish Schools	Destrehan, LA
Substitute Teacher	August 2014-May 2015

Assisted special education students in schoolwork and recreation activities; completed individualized student plans and tracking charts; and coordinated with parents to implement student-specific goals.

SKILLS & INTERESTS

(1) Languages: French (Limited Working Proficiency) and Spanish (Elementary Proficiency)
(2) Alto - Gospel Choir

Notes:

1. Stacy used the U.S. Department of State's language proficiency definitions to describe her language proficiency. She plans to practice international law, so this is the correct way to note such proficiency.

2. The addition of Stacy's interest in singing, especially the specific type of music, provides an Employer with something to discuss with her in an interview.

Checklist: Special Skills and Interests

Languages:	Yes	No
Do you speak another language?		
Is your additional language an asset but not a requirement for the job?		
If yes, have you described your language skills using generally understood terms, such as conversational or fluent?		
Is your additional language required for the job?		
If yes, have you described your fluency using the U.S. Department of State standards?		
If you are an international student and plan to work outside the U.S., have you described your English fluency using the U.S. Department of State standards?		
Computer Skills:		
Do you possess specialized computer skills that would be an asset for the job (not standard computer skills such as Excel, Lexis, Westlaw, Word, etc.)?		
If yes, have you included those specialized computer skills in this section of your resume?		
If those specialized computer skills are important to your future legal practice and you are "certified" in the use of such skills, have you included that certification in the "Education" section of your resume?		
Interests:		
Do you have an interest or skill in music, dance, theatre, athletics, cooking, etc.?		
If so, have you included that interest in a way that is specific to you (Cuban cooking, Latin dance, etc.)?		
Proofing:		
Is the font consistent with the rest of your resume?		
Is this section formatted consistently with the rest of your resume?		
Are there any proofing errors (misspelled words, incorrect punctuation, etc.)?		

Part II

Cover Letters

Chapter 7

Purpose and Logistics: Why Do I Need a Cover Letter and What Do I Put in It?

Now that your resume is done, it is time to send it to an Employer. To do that properly, you need to draft a cover letter.

Purpose of Cover Letters

The purpose of a cover letter is to introduce you to an Employer. It gives you the opportunity to make a connection to that Employer before the Employer reads your resume and learns about your skills and accomplishments. A cover letter is also the first writing sample an Employer will read, even before your resume, and needs to reflect your excellent writing skills. It should be concise, clear and convincing, and it ought to complement, not repeat, your resume.

The good news is that you have drafted cover letters before. Prior to law school, you drafted them for applications, as well as wrote thank-you letters; in law school, you may have drafted advisory or settlement letters. The cover letter you write to an Employer is actually a mini-advisory letter: in it you are advising or persuading the Employer to read your resume closely and then offer you an interview.

Because you are unique, your cover letter should be unique. Therefore, you do not want to use a form cover letter from a booklet provided by your career services office or a website. When students ask me to review their cover letters, I know from the first sentence if it is from a form booklet, because it sounds so generic. Keep in mind that many of your classmates may be applying to the same Employer, especially if the Employer is participating in a school-related interview program. The last thing you want is for that Employer to see you as just another applicant and not the standout that you are. (This is especially true for students who are applying for judicial internships and clerkships.) While the sample letters your career services office provides are useful as samples (as are the sample cover letters included in this book), they are just that — samples. They were not written by you or for you, and therefore can't possibly create a connection with an Employer like the cover letter you will draft after reading the next few chapters.

Should I Always Send a Cover Letter?

The answer is YES, with one exception I'll discuss below. Otherwise, always send a cover letter, including when you submit your resume for a school-sponsored, on-campus interview program.

Many students do not prepare a cover letter for these programs, which is a mistake for several reasons. First, you are missing an opportunity to make a connection to an Employer and to demonstrate your excellent writing skills. Second, you are missing an opportunity to "make your case" for why the Employer should interview you. If you are one of the few students who do include a cover letter, you will stand out as someone who went the extra mile to make a good impression.

The only time you do not want to include a cover letter with your resume is if an Employer specifically asks students not to include one. In that case, if you do include a cover letter, then you are not following the Employer's directions and will likely get eliminated from consideration on that basis.

Logistics/Format

Your cover letter should follow standard business format, and be no longer than one page. As noted in Chapter 1, use the same font for your cover letter that you used for your resume. Generally, 12-point Times New Roman is appropriate. Margins must be at least one inch on each side. Most attorneys and legal organizations use white paper and if you want to look like one of them, you will, too. Many years ago, students were advised to use off-white or crème-colored paper for cover letters, but this is not current practice. The content of your cover letter will make you stand out, not the paper color.

Email vs. Hard Copy

The format is the same whether you send your cover letter via email or hard copy. If you send your letter via email, to make it look like a letter, send it as a PDF attachment. (In Chapter 11, you will learn how to include your signature in a PDF.) When sending your letter as an attachment via email, include your connection to the Employer in the subject matter of the email to insure that the recipient opens and reads it. Do not put something like "Internship Applicant" or anything job-related unless the posting requires application materials be sent via email. In the latter case, you can use the internship posting number or title of position in the subject matter line of your message.

Sections of Cover Letter

Your cover letter will have the following sections, in this order: Heading, Addressee, Introduction, Facts, Discussion/Argument, and Closing. If these words look familiar to you, they should. You included each of these sections in every memo, letter, and brief you drafted or will draft in law school and as an attorney. Sometimes, these sections are called by different names; however, the substance is always the same. The following chapters in this book discuss each of these sections in detail.

Before we move forward, let's take a look at some *before* and *after* cover letters. These letters are grouped according to the following types of situations:

1. School connection to an Employer (e.g., on- or off-campus interview or networking programs);
2. Non-school connection to an Employer; and
3. Weak or no connection to an Employer.

As you review each of the following cover letters, ask yourself: "Whose resume will you read?" and "Whom would you invite for an interview?"

Chapter 7

Sample Cover Letters

Cover Letter — Purpose and Logistics

Before

Sample cover letter of Denise Hollander (school connection).

DENISE ALYSSA HOLLANDER

1234 West Pine Blvd #10L • St. Louis, MO 63108

dahollander@wustl.edu

(941) 123-4567

January 14, 20XX

Ms. Marsha Dennis
Tucker Smith LLP
7000 Forsyth Blvd, Ste 1000
St. Louis, MO 63105

Dear Ms. Dennis:

I am a first-year Dean's Fellow at Washington University School of Law and am interested in a summer associate position with Tucker Smith in 20XX. I moved to St. Louis this past summer and am eager to gain experience in the St. Louis legal community, as I am planning to make St. Louis my permanent home. I am interested in exploring your firm's wide variety of practice areas, especially the firm's growing intellectual property practice area, and am excited by the opportunity to seek responsibility early on as an associate.

I am confident that I have the work ethic and enthusiasm to be an asset to Tucker Smith this summer and beyond. In addition to maintaining a strong overall academic record, ranking in the top XX% of my class, I have demonstrated my writing ability by earning the highest grade in my Legal Practice course, X.X. This builds on my prior research and writing experience obtained through journalistic training at the University of South Florida and as a media fellow for multiple organizations. Moreover, I developed leadership skills while serving as vice president of USF Hillel, a Jewish campus organization, during which time I led executive student board meetings and worked in close partnership with the student president. I welcome the opportunity to apply and hone those skills while collaborating with team members at Tucker Smith.

Thank you for your time and consideration. I hope to have the opportunity to demonstrate why I am a great fit for your firm during an on-campus interview. In the meantime, please feel free to contact me at the telephone number or e-mail address listed above.

Sincerely,

Denise A. Hollander

After

Edited sample cover letter of Denise Hollander (school connection).

DENISE ALYSSA HOLLANDER
1234 West Pine Blvd #10L • St. Louis, MO 63108
dahollander@wustl.edu
(941) 123-4567

January 14, 20XX

Ms. Marsha Dennis
Tucker Smith LLP
7000 Forsyth Blvd
Suite 1000
St. Louis, MO 63105

Dear Ms. Dennis:

I recently spoke with John Holmes, one of your intellectual property attorneys, at the Employer Showcase hosted by Washington University School of Law ("Wash U Law"). I also had the opportunity to attend the 1L reception hosted by Tucker Smith in December. The collaborative and welcoming atmosphere of your firm was evident to me from both of those experiences. As a recent transplant to St. Louis, I am eager to make a connection in the St. Louis legal community with a firm like yours that has a varied, sophisticated practice as well as a reputation for community engagement. Please accept this letter and my attached resume as my application for a summer internship with Tucker Smith.

I am interested in exploring your firm's wide variety of practice areas, especially intellectual property, and am excited by the opportunity to seek responsibility early on as an associate. I am confident that I have the research and writing skills, leadership skills, and enthusiasm to be an asset to Tucker Smith this summer and beyond. In addition to maintaining a strong overall academic record, ranking in the top XX% of my class, I have demonstrated my writing ability in law school by earning the highest grade in my Legal Practice course, X.X. This builds on my prior research and writing experience obtained through journalistic training at the University of South Florida and as a media fellow for multiple organizations. Moreover, I developed leadership skills while serving in a variety of capacities at my undergraduate university and in the South Florida community. In addition to building a successful legal practice, it is important to me to be involved in my community. Tucker Smith's demonstrated commitment to the St. Louis community appeals to me.

I understand that Tucker Smith is participating in the on-campus interview program at Wash U Law and I welcome the opportunity to meet with you or one of your colleagues. In the meantime, please contact me if there is any other information you need from me at this time.

Sincerely,

Denise Hollander

Denise Hollander

Encl.: resume

Before

Sample cover letter of Timothy Newstead (non-school connection).

Timothy J. Newstead
7424 Buckingham Dr., Apt. 2D
St. Louis, MO 63105

January 12, 20XX

Ms. Jane Allen
101 Second Street, Suite 600
San Francisco, CA 94105

Dear Ms. Allen:

I am a first-year law student at Washington University in St. Louis School of Law. I am writing to express my interest in the internship position for the California Appellate Project this summer.

My primary reason for choosing to attend law school was so that I could become a public defender. My desire to work in California has led me to apply for this position. I am currently a member of the Public Service Advisory Board at Washington University. PSAB is a student-led organization that allocates public service funds among student groups, facilitates educational events about public service careers, creates opportunities for public service within the law school and in the larger St. Louis community, and administers the Pro Bono Pledge. I am a member of the Public Service Committee, which organizes service projects to foster student involvement with the community. I believe that my involvement with this organization has strengthened my determination to pursue a career in public service.

While I have not received my final grades for the first semester, I anticipate that I will have a solid GPA. I received high marks for papers in Legal Practice I and Criminal Law. I graduated from the University of Notre Dame in 2012 with a Bachelor of Science degree. I spent my last two years at Notre Dame volunteering as an after-school tutor for local youth and volunteering at a local hospital once a week. I believe that my commitment to service can be seen through these activities, as well as the year I spent living in Jamaica with the Passionist Volunteers International. I believe that spending the upcoming summer as an intern for the California Appellate Project would be an incredible opportunity and the first-step in realizing my goal of becoming a public defender.

I will be in Chicago during the weekend of February 6th for the Midwest Public Interest Law Career Conference. I would welcome the opportunity to meet with you during the conference to discuss the summer internship. Please feel free to contact me anytime at (314) 123-4567 or newsteadt@wustl.edu. Thank you in advance for your consideration.
Sincerely,

Timothy J. Newstead

After

Edited sample cover letter of Timothy Newstead (non-school connection).

Timothy J. Newstead
7424 Buckingham Dr., Apt. 2D
St. Louis, MO 63105

January 12, 20XX

Jane Allen, Esquire
California Appellate Project
101 Second Street, Suite 600
San Francisco, CA 94105

Dear Ms. Allen:

Sarah Volk, my friend and a former intern with the California Appellate Project (the "Appellate Project"), recommended that I apply for the 20XX summer internship. Sarah's enthusiasm for the work she did at the Appellate Project as an intern last summer inspired me to apply for an internship this summer. I am a first-year law student at Washington University in St. Louis School of Law. Like Sarah, I am committed to a career in public interest law, with an emphasis on criminal law. Please accept this letter and my enclosed resume as my application for a summer internship with the Appellate Project.

My primary goal in attending law school is to work in criminal defense, perhaps as a public defender. I am currently a member of the Public Service Advisory Board at Washington University. PSAB is a student-led organization that allocates public service funds among student groups, facilitates educational events about public service careers, creates opportunities for public service within the law school and in the larger St. Louis community, and administers the Pro Bono Pledge. I am an active member of the Public Service Committee and have had the opportunity to organize service projects to foster student involvement with the St. Louis community. My involvement with this organization has strengthened my determination to pursue a career in public service.

My commitment to public service predates law school. I spent my last two years at Notre Dame volunteering as an after-school tutor for local youth and weekly at a local hospital. I also spent a year after college living and working in Jamaica with the Passionist Volunteers International. My interest in criminal law stems from the challenges I observed many of my students enduring as their family members navigated the criminal justice system, often without consistent legal representation. I believe that spending this summer as an intern for the Appellate Project would be an incredible opportunity and the first step in realizing my goal of becoming a public defender.

I will be in Chicago during the weekend of February 6th for the Midwest Public Interest Law Career Conference, and welcome the opportunity to meet with you or one of your colleagues to discuss the Appellate Project and my qualifications for an internship with it. In the meantime, please feel free to contact me at (314) 123-4567 or newsteadt@wustl.edu. Thank you in advance for your consideration.

Sincerely,

Timothy J. Newstead

Timothy J. Newstead

Encl.: Resume

Before

Sample cover letter of Frank Douglas (weak or no connection).

Dear Mr. Winston,

I am a first-year student at Washington University School of Law, and I am writing to express my interest in the 1L summer internship offered by the EPA's Philadelphia office. My main goal in applying to law school was to eventually find a job in the field of environmental law. My interest in environmental issues began in college, where I took classes on the environmental consequences of globalization, the philosophical problems of climate change, and the rational choice theory behind international negotiations on environmental agreements. Since my undergraduate years, my desire to work in the environmental field has only grown stronger. As a first-year law student I have not yet had the opportunity to take any classes in environmental law, but I have dedicated my personal time to working with Washington University's Energy and Environmental Law Society (EELS) as an elected board member. In that capacity, I've both learned more about climate change and broadened the scope of my interest to include other environmental problems. The state of the environment strikes me as one of the most critical issues facing the world right now, and I believe that spending my career working on environmental issues would bring me more professional fulfillment than working in any other practice area. I believe that this position at the EPA presents an incredible opportunity to learn about the type of work that environmental lawyers do.

In my first semester of law school, I performed especially well in Contracts and Legal Research. I believe that the attention to detail and the precise thinking required for Contracts classes would be a useful asset to a 1L intern. Furthermore, if I am asked to do any research, the skills I have learned in my Legal Research class will surely help me to be a more successful intern. I am a fast learner, and will work hard to pick up any skills necessary to be useful to your office as an intern. I feel that with this range of qualities I have the ability to be a productive member of your office despite my lack of professional legal experience.

If you have any questions, please feel free to contact me at (609) 123-4567 or fddouglas@wustl.edu. Thank you for your time and consideration.

Sincerely,

Frank D. Douglas

After

Edited sample cover letter of Frank Douglas (weak or no connection).

Frank D. Douglas

1234 Lindell Blvd., Apt. W-504   (609) 123-4567
St. Louis, MO 63108   fddouglas@wustl.edu

January 25, 20XX

Mr. Thomas Winston
U.S. Environmental Protection Agency
Region III (3RC00)
1650 Arch Street
Philadelphia, PA 19103-2029

Dear Mr. Winston,

As a first-year student at Washington University School of Law ("Law School"), I am writing to express my interest in the Legal Internship ("Internship") at the Environmental Protection Agency ("EPA") office in Philadelphia. Past participants and fellow law students, Roseanne Brown and John Caruthers, recommended that I apply.

My lifelong interest in environmental issues, research skills, and ability to communicate would make me an effective EPA intern. My interest in the environment, particularly climate change, is one of the reasons I decided to attend law school. As an attorney, I want to use my passion and legal knowledge to impact policies that will benefit future generations. As an undergraduate, I studied the environmental consequences of globalization, philosophical problems of climate change, and rational choice theory behind international environmental agreements. While I have not had the opportunity as a first-year law student to take environmental law classes, I have dedicated my personal time to working with the Law School's Energy and Environmental Law Society as an elected board member. In that capacity, I have learned more about climate change and broadened the scope of my interest in environmental issues. I earned one of my highest grades this past semester in legal research, and am anxious to put that skill into practice in the environmental area. Prior to law school I taught English as a Second Language as part of a ministry program. As a teacher, I learned to communicate effectively with supervisors and students. My passion for the environment, research ability and communication skills would be an asset to the EPA.

I will be in the Philadelphia area in March and welcome the opportunity to meet with you or one of your colleagues then to learn more about the Internship and share my thoughts on why I would be an asset to the program. I will contact you in a few weeks to confirm that you received this letter and my enclosed resume and to see if there is a convenient time for us to meet in March. In the meantime, if you have any questions, please contact me. Thank you for your consideration.

Sincerely,

Frank D. Douglas
Frank D. Douglas

Encl.: Resume

Checklist: Cover Letter — Purpose and Logistics

Logistics:	Yes	No
Did you begin the format of your letter using the same font as your resume?		
Did you use white paper, the same as your resume, if you are sending a hard copy?		
Email vs. Hard Copy:		
If you are sending your letter via email, did you include your connection in the subject matter of the email?		
If you are sending your letter via email, did you include the letter as a PDF attachment with your signature?		

Chapter 8

Heading, Addressee, and Introduction: Who Are You and Why Are You Writing This Cover Letter?

Your cover letter begins with a Heading, then the name of the Addressee: the person and organization to whom you are writing. The Introduction, which follows, is the first substantive section of your cover letter.

Purpose of Section

Like your resume, every section of your cover letter tells an Employer something about you. Your cover letter should start off strongly so that an Employer immediately becomes interested in you and your resume.

Step-by-Step Guide

Heading

The Heading on a cover letter is similar to the Heading on your resume, which includes identifying information (see Chapter 2): your name, address or addresses, email, and cell phone number. However, for the Heading on your cover letter, you only need your name, email, and cell phone number. A permanent or school address is not necessary; most Employers communicate by email or phone, and if they want to communicate with you via regular mail, your address is on your resume.

Date

Include the date on your cover letter above the Addressee. The date is placed either on the left, using the same margin as the Addressee, or on the far right; this is a matter of personal preference. Use standard format for writing the date (i.e., do not include a "th" after the day):

Proper Format: January 5, 2017
Improper Format: January 5th, 2017

Addressee

The Addressee includes the name, title, and address of the person to whom you are writing. Use the name of a particular person and not an organization or department, such as "Human Resources." This may require you to do some research, but it's worth it. Letters sent to offices or departments are impersonal. To make a connection with an Employer, address your cover letter to a specific person.

If the person to whom you are addressing the letter is an attorney, use the person's name with "Esquire" after it. In the salutation, however, use the title of "Mr." or "Ms." without "Esquire." If the person to whom you are addressing the letter has an honorific (for example, a judge), use the appropriate honorific rather than "Mr." or "Ms." Note that when addressing a letter to a judge, you do not include Esquire after the judge's name in the first line of the address. Here are some examples:

Addressee who is not an attorney:

> Ms. Jane D. Smith
> Director of Attorney Recruiting
> (name of organization and address)

> Dear Ms. Smith,

Addressee who is an attorney:

> Susan M. Lewis, Esquire
> Hiring Partner
> (name of organization and address)

> Dear Ms. Lewis,

Addressee who may or may not be an attorney with an honorific:

> The Honorable Catherine D. Perry
> United States District Court for the Eastern District of Missouri
> (address)

> Dear Judge Perry,

Introduction

The first paragraph of your cover letter is your first opportunity to establish a relationship with an Employer; in it, you tell the Addressee who you are and why you are writing the letter. The Introduction is only about two or three sentences long, but it can encourage or discourage an Employer from reading the rest of your letter and your resume. Do not start with the standard sentence used in too many cover letters: "I am a first-year student at XYZ law school and am interested in applying for a summer internship with your organization." You can do better.

For example, before writing the Introduction, determine the nature of your connection to an Employer. In general, there are three potential types of connection: 1) school-related (e.g., from an on-campus or off-campus interview program or networking event); 2) non-school-related; or 3) weak or none. This last scenario is the least fruitful for students, so I encourage you to look very hard to find a connection. This may mean that you need to find out if anyone at your law school knows someone at a particular Employer's. Once that connection is determined, put it in your first sentence. A name or event will grab Employers' attention and encourage them to keep reading.

The second piece of information you should include is the reason you sent the cover letter. Perhaps it's required as part of an application; maybe you sent it as a follow-up to an Employer's networking event, or in anticipation of a program in which an Employer is a participant. Whatever the reason for the letter, say what it is in your first or second sentence; don't leave an Employer trying to figure it out. Finally, to encourage an Employer to interview you, say that you would appreciate the opportunity to meet that Employer in person.

Additional Tips for International Students

If you included information on your resume establishing your legal authority to work in the U.S., also include that information in the Introduction of your cover letter. Employers want to know that you are legally able to work with them. Name the type of visa you hold that permits you to work in the U.S.

Chapter 8

Sample Cover Letters

Heading, Addressee, and Introduction

Sample 8.1

Before

Cover letter of Matthew Novack (school connection).

Notes:

1. Matthew includes only his school address and not his target area address.

2. It is unclear whether or not the addressee is an attorney.

3. The addressee's position with the CFTC is not included.

4. Matthew starts out his letter with the typical "I am a first year law student" language rather than noting his connection to the Employer. He did note the specific internship he is applying for.

Matthew T. Novack
① 7025 Forsyth Dr.
St. Louis, MO 63105
(845) 123-4567
mtnovack@wustl.edu

January 24, 20XX

② Mr. Benjamin Cruse
③ Commodity Futures Trading Commission
140 Broadway
New York, NY 10005

Dear Mr. Cruse,

④ I am a first year law student at Washington University in St. Louis writing to apply for the Commodity Futures Trading Commission's 20XX Summer Internship Program.

I am pursuing a career in securities litigation and white collar criminal prosecution. A position as a summer intern at the CFTC will provide me with an unparalleled opportunity to pursue these interests and apply my own corporate experience in a way that will contribute substantively to the Commission's efforts.

During my first semester of law school, I excelled in all of my classes and I received the highest grade in my torts class of approximately 80 students. Overall, my GPA places me on the Dean's List and in the top XX% of my grade. My success this semester is a testament to the ambition I will bring to the CFTC.

Prior to law school I worked as a market research analyst for a business information firm called Avention, where I researched corporate information technology trends and immersed myself in financial statements and SEC filings using the SEC's EDGAR database. I compiled reports on information technology and corporate expenditures in a variety of industries, using U.S. Census Bureau economic data and American FactFinder to extrapolate trends and identify growth areas. My technical understanding of corporate underpinnings is a great asset to any securities litigator or white collar prosecutor, and I know it will serve me well at the CFTC.

Please feel free to contact me at (845) 123-4567 or mtnovack@wustl.edu if you have any questions. Thank you in advance for your time and consideration. I look forward to hearing from you

Sincerely,

Matthew T. Novack

After

Edited cover letter of Matthew Novack (school connection).

Matthew T. Novack
(845) 123-4567
mtnovack@wustl.edu

School Address
7025 Forsyth Dr.
St. Louis, MO 63105

❶ Permanent Address
16 Adams Court
Nanuet, NY 10954

January 24, 20XX

❷ Benjamin Cruse, Esquire
Commodity Futures Trading Commission
140 Broadway
New York, NY 10005

❸ RE: 20XX Summer Internship Program

Dear Mr. Cruse,

Please accept the enclosed resume and personal statement as my application for the Commodity Futures Trading Commission's ("CFTC's") 20XX Summer Internship Program ("Internship"). I **❹** learned about the CFTC Internship at the Federal Government Career Fair held at my law school, Washington University in St. Louis–School of Law. I was intrigued by the opportunities that participants in the CFTC Internship have to participate in all phases of the CFTC's work. After **❺** law school, I plan to use my background in corporate work and psychology to pursue a career in securities litigation and white-collar criminal prosecution. If selected for the CFTC Internship, I welcome the opportunity to pursue my interests and to apply my corporate experience and expertise in securities research to contribute substantively to the CFTC's efforts.

Prior to law school, I worked as a market research analyst for a business information firm, where I researched corporate information technology trends and immersed myself in financial statements and SEC filings using the SEC's EDGAR database. I drafted reports on information technology and corporate expenditures in a variety of industries, using U.S. Census Bureau economic data and American FactFinder to extrapolate trends and identify growth areas. I believe that my technical understanding of corporate underpinnings and securities research experience will allow me to assist you and your colleagues at the CFTC this summer.

I welcome the opportunity to speak with you or one of your colleagues about my interest in, and qualifications for, the CFTC Internship program. I will contact you in a couple of weeks to confirm receipt of my application materials. In the meantime, please contact me at (845) 123-4567 or mtnovack@wustl.edu if you have any questions. Thank you in advance for your time and consideration.

Sincerely,

Matthew T. Novack
Matthew T. Novack

Encls.: Resume
            Statement of Interest

Notes:

1. Matthew added his address in New York. This shows Matthew's connection to the area.

---

2. The addressee is an attorney and therefore "Esquire" was added after his name. The addressee does not have a specific position with the Employer so there is no title to include.

---

3. The subject matter of the letter was included.

---

4. Matthew noted his school connection to the Employer.

---

5. Matthew explained why he is applying for this specific internship and how he believes he could contribute to the Employer.

Sample 8.3

Before

Cover letter of Carrie Yu (non-school connection).

Notes:

1. Carrie includes all relevant information in the heading.

2. She includes the addressee's title. She needs to add a "Ms." before the addressee's name.

3. Carrie starts her letter with the typical "I am a first-year student" rather than stating her connection to the Employer. Her connection is noted at the very end of the paragraph and should be included earlier.

❶ Carrie S. Yu
12 South Kingshighway Blvd., Apt. 12S
St. Louis, MO 63108
(703) 123-4567
carriesyu@wustl.edu

December 18, 20XX

❷ Valerie Rogers
Senior Manager, Recruiting & Retention
Davis Smith P.C.
1234 Main Street
Indianapolis, IN 46204

Dear Ms. Rogers,

❸ I am a first-year student at Washington University School of Law and I hope to be considered for a 1L Summer Associate position at the New York Office of Davis Smith. I worked in New York for two years before attending law school and hope to return to the area after graduation. I am specifically interested in working for Davis Smith because I admire the firm's impressive labor and employment practice. Furthermore, having chatted extensively with Sarah Jones at the National Asian Pacific American Bar Association Conference in New Orleans this November, I truly admire Davis Smith's dedication to diversity.

I believe I am the ideal candidate for this position for a number of reasons. Having worked as a Research Assistant for both the Government and Psychology Departments at Georgetown as well as the Psychology Department at University College London, I have the research and writing skills necessary to be a successful associate. Furthermore, having worked as a Litigation Paralegal at Paul Weiss for the two years prior to law school, I know that my attention to detail, perfectionist personality, and strong work ethic are characteristics that will allow me to succeed in the fast paced environment of Davis Smith.

I plan to be in New York during the first week of January and I am able to take a quick train up to the city at any time between now and January 8th when I return to St. Louis for school. I would greatly appreciate the opportunity to meet with someone in the New York Office to discuss how I can be an asset to Davis Smith. I look forward to hearing from you.

Sincerely,

Carrie S. Yu

Sample 8.4

After

Edited cover letter of Carrie Yu (non-school connection).

Carrie S. Yu
12 South Kingshighway Blvd., Apt. 12S
St. Louis, MO 63108
(703) 123-4567
carriesyu@wustl.edu

December 18, 20XX

1 Ms. Valerie Rogers
Senior Manager, Recruiting & Retention
Davis Smith P.C.
1234 Main Street
Indianapolis, IN 46204

2 RE: Davis Smith New York Internship

Dear Ms. Rogers,

3 I met Sarah Jones from your firm's New York office at the National Asian Pacific American Bar Association Conference in New Orleans this November, and she encouraged me to apply for a 1L summer associate position in the firm's New York office. Ms. Jones's enthusiasm for her labor and employment practice at Davis Smith, as well as the firm's demonstrated dedication to diversity, is very appealing to me. I worked in New York for two years before attending law school and plan to return to the area after graduation. I believe I am a very strong candidate for a summer associate position with your firm for a number of reasons.

My research and writing skills, prior work experience, and ability to work in a fast-paced environment will be assets in this position. This fall, at the end of my first semester in law school, I received the highest grade in my Legal Practice (research and writing) section. This grade was based on multiple research and writing assignments. For the two years prior to law school, I worked as a Litigation Paralegal at a large, sophisticated New York City law firm. In that position, I supervised a team of paralegals in connection with a nationwide class-action lawsuit involving thousands of documents. I know that my attention to detail, perfectionist personality, and strong work ethic are characteristics that will allow me to succeed in the fast-paced environment of Davis Smith.

I will be in New York during the first week of January and welcome the opportunity to meet with you or your colleagues to discuss my qualifications for a summer associate position with Davis Smith. I will contact you in a couple of weeks to confirm that you received this letter and my enclosed resume. In the meantime, please let me know if you need additional information from me. Thank you in advance for your consideration.

Sincerely,

Carrie S. Yu

Encl.: resume

Notes:

1. Carrie added "Ms." before the addressee's name.

---

2. Carrie added the subject matter of her letter so the addressee knows the office that Carrie is interested in.

---

3. Carrie stated her connection to the Employer immediately, including where and when she made that connection. She stated the reason she is interested in working with this Employer.

Sample 8.5

Before

Cover letter of Frank Douglas (weak or no connection).

Notes:

1. Frank needs to add a heading, date, and the addressee's information.

2. Frank starts with the typical first-year law student language. Even though he may not have a strong connection to the Employer, Frank needs to try to find one.

3. The first paragraph of his letter is too long and contains too much information, making it difficult to follow.

❶

Dear Mr. Winston,

❷ I am a first-year student at Washington University School of Law, and I am writing to express my interest in the 1L summer internship offered by the EPA's Philadelphia office.

❸ My main goal in applying to law school was to eventually find a job in the field of environmental law. My interest in environmental issues began in college, where I took classes on the environmental consequences of globalization, the philosophical problems of climate change, and the rational choice theory behind international negotiations on environmental agreements. Since my undergraduate years, my desire to work in the environmental field has only grown stronger. As a first-year law student I have not yet had the opportunity to take any classes in environmental law, but I have dedicated my personal time to working with Washington University's Energy and Environmental Law Society (EELS) as an elected board member. In that capacity, I've both learned more about climate change and broadened the scope of my interest to include other environmental problems. The state of the environment strikes me as one of the most critical issues facing the world right now, and I believe that spending my career working on environmental issues would bring me more professional fulfillment than working in any other practice area. I believe that this position at the EPA presents an incredible opportunity to learn about the type of work that environmental lawyers do.

In my first semester of law school, I performed especially well in Contracts and Legal Research. I believe that the attention to detail and the precise thinking required for Contracts classes would be a useful asset to a 1L intern. Furthermore, if I am asked to do any research, the skills I have learned in my Legal Research class will surely help me to be a more successful intern. I am a fast learner, and will work hard to pick up any skills necessary to be useful to your office as an intern. I feel that with this range of qualities I have the ability to be a productive member of your office despite my lack of professional legal experience.

If you have any questions, please feel free to contact me at (609) 123-4567 or fddouglas@wustl.edu. Thank you for your time and consideration.

Sincerely,

Frank D. Douglas

Sample 8.6

After

Edited cover letter of Frank Douglas (weak or no connection).

Frank D. Douglas

❶ 1234 Lindell Blvd., Apt. W-504   (609) 123-4567
St. Louis, MO 63108   fddouglas@wustl.edu

January 25, 20XX

Mr. Thomas Winston
U.S. Environmental Protection Agency
Region III (3RC00)
1650 Arch Street
Philadelphia, PA 19103-2029

Dear Mr. Winston,

❷   As a first-year student at Washington University School of Law ("Law School"), I am writing to express my interest in the Legal Internship ("Internship") at the Environmental Protection Agency ("EPA") office in Philadelphia. Past participants and fellow law students, Roseanne Brown and John Caruthers, recommended that I apply.

My lifelong interest in environmental issues, research skills, and ability to communicate would make me an effective EPA intern. My interest in the environment, particularly climate change, is one of the reasons I decided to attend law school. As an attorney, I want to use my passion and legal knowledge to impact policies that will benefit future generations. As an undergraduate, I studied the environmental consequences of globalization, philosophical problems of climate change, and rational choice theory behind international environmental agreements. While I have not had the opportunity as a first-year law student to take environmental law classes, I have dedicated my personal time to working with the Law School's Energy and Environmental Law Society as an elected board member. In that capacity, I have learned more about climate change and broadened the scope of my interest in environmental issues. I earned one of my highest grades this past semester in legal research, and am anxious to put that skill into practice in the environmental area. Prior to law school I taught English as a Second Language as part of a ministry program. As a teacher, I learned to communicate effectively with supervisors and students. My passion for the environment, research ability and communication skills would be an asset to the EPA.

I will be in the Philadelphia area in March and welcome the opportunity to meet with you or one of your colleagues then to learn more about the Internship and share my thoughts on why I would be an asset to the program. I will contact you in a few weeks to confirm that you received this letter and my enclosed resume and to see if there is a convenient time for us to meet in March. In the meantime, if you have any questions, please contact me. Thank you for your consideration.

Sincerely,

Frank D. Douglas
Frank D. Douglas

Encl.: Resume

Notes:

1. Frank added a heading, date, and information about the addressee.

---

2. In the first sentence, Frank noted the purpose of his letter. In the second sentence, he noted his connection to the Employer: two fellow students who worked at the office last year. In the first paragraph, Frank included defined terms that he will use later in his letter.

Checklist: Cover Letter — Heading, Addressee, and Introduction

Heading:	Yes	No
Did you include your name, email, and cell phone number at the top of your letter?		
If your target city is not the city in which your law school is located, did you include an address in that target city (i.e., permanent address) in your heading in addition to your school address?		
Date:		
Did you include the date you are sending the letter?		
Did you include the date alone without a "th" after it?		
Addressee:		
Is your letter addressed to a specific person?		
Did you double-check the spelling of the addressee's name?		
Did you include that person's title?		
If the addressee is an attorney, did you leave out the "Mr." or "Ms." and use "Esquire" after his or her name?		
If the addressee is not a lawyer, did you include a "Mr." or "Ms." before his or her name?		
If the addressee has an honorific (i.e., a judge or senator), did you include the honorific before his or her name?		
Introduction:		
Did you begin your letter by identifying your connection to the Employer?		
Did you tell the addressee why you are writing the letter?		
Did you identify yourself as a law student and an applicant for a position with the Employer?		
Did you tell the addressee that you would appreciate the opportunity to meet a representative of the Employer in person?		
Proofing:		
Is the font for the Heading, Addressee, and Introduction consistent with your resume?		
Is the Introduction formatted consistently with the rest of your letter (i.e., indented the same number of spaces, spacing between lines)?		
Are there any proofing errors (misspelled words, including names, incorrect punctuation, etc.)?		

Chapter 9

Facts: What Are One or Two Things That You Want Me to Know About You?

Purpose of Section

The Facts paragraph presents an opportunity for you to highlight your individuality in a personal and professional way. In it, convey one or two things about yourself that might not be evident from your resume and that will be of interest to an Employer. Do not simply repeat your resume. Sometimes, this paragraph can be combined with the Introduction or the Discussion/Argument section of your letter (see Chapter 10).

Step-by-Step Guide

The goal of this section is to provide specific facts that show your strengths and uniqueness, and to lead into a discussion of why you would be a good fit for an Employer's practice. First, before drafting this paragraph, make a list of facts you might include—for example, a geographic connection to an Employer, relevant undergraduate studies and work experience, or academic achievements in law school. Some types of phrases you might use to describe yourself are:

"lifelong New Yorker"
"lifelong Midwesterner"
"former chemical engineer"
"urban planning major"
"committed community organizer"

Second, state the facts in a conversational and professional manner. One way to do this is to pretend that you are introducing yourself to an Employer for the first time and put those words into writing. Third, include a sentence or two noting your goals and tying those goals into the reason you would like to work with that particular Employer. Finally, use the facts to lead into the next section of your letter: the Discussion/Argument of why you are a good fit for that Employer. Facts that dovetail with your Discussion/Argument are more persuasive than facts that stand alone.

Chapter 9

Sample Cover Letters

Facts

Sample 9.1

Before

Cover letter of Laura Mackey (school connection).

Notes:

1. Laura notes that she did well academically in two classes at law school but does not include the specifics of such achievements.

2. Laura reiterates the work she did prior to law school and begins to relate it to the Employer's practice.

3. She includes a general statement about her passion for this area of law.

Laura M. Mackey
123 Westgate Ave #6
St. Louis, Missouri 63130 lmm@wustl.edu

January 10, 20XX

Missouri State Public Defender System
Attn: Human Resources
Woodrail Centre
1000 West Nifong, Building 7, Suite 100
Columbia, Missouri 65203

Dear Missouri State Public Defender Office,

I am a first year student at the Washington University School of Law and am interested in a summer position at the Missouri State Public Defenders office for this coming summer. I am committed to staying in the St. Louis area this summer, but am willing to commute if there is a greater need for an intern in a different location.

I am confident that my experience and enthusiasm will contribute to your office. My academic achievements at Washington University include high grades in Criminal Law as well as Legal Practice in which I earned high grades on my writing assignments. Prior to Washington University, I worked for the Santa Barbara Superior Court's Own Recognizance Unit. In this position I interviewed individuals just after arrest with the aim of releasing them from custody without having to pay bail. While our primary task was to reduce jail population, my office was often able to help individuals who would not otherwise be able to post bail. During my time in this office, I gained an understanding of the criminal legal process. I also witnessed the impact this process can have on low-income individuals and their families. It was this experience that inspired the passion I believe I can bring to your office.

Please feel free to contact me at (805) 123-4567. Thank you in advance for your consideration. I look forward to speaking with you.

Sincerely,

Laura M. Mackey

Sample 9.2

After

Edited cover letter of Laura Mackey (school connection).

Laura M. Mackey
123 Westgate Ave #6
St. Louis, Missouri 63130 lmm@wustl.edu

January 10, 20XX

Missouri State Public Defender System
Attn: Gina Hall, Human Resources
Woodrail Centre
1000 West Nifong, Building 7, Suite 100
Columbia, Missouri 65203

Dear Ms. Hall,

A representative from the Missouri State Public Defender's Office (the "PD Office") spoke at Washington University School of Law's Public Service Career Fair this week. At that event, I talked to Mr. David Sanger, a public defender with your office. Mr. Sanger's enthusiasm for his work inspired me to seek an internship with the PD Office. As a first year law student I am hoping to combine my new legal skills with my experience working in the criminal justice system by working for your office this coming summer. I plan to live in the St. Louis area, but am willing to commute to another city if there is a greater need for an intern in a different location.

I am confident that my academic achievements, experience, and enthusiasm will contribute to the PD Office. This first year of law school, I am proud to have earned high grades in Criminal Law and Legal Practice, our legal analysis and writing course. In Legal Practice, ❶ I received praise for my research-based writing assignments and my oral presentation skills. ❷ Prior to law school, I worked for the Santa Barbara Superior Court Recognizance Unit. I interviewed individuals immediately after arrest with the goal of releasing them from custody without bail. While our primary task was to reduce jail population, my office was often able to help individuals who would not otherwise be able to post bail. During my time in this position, I gained an understanding of the criminal legal process. I also witnessed the impact this process can have on low-income individuals and their families. It ❸ was this experience that inspired the passion I will bring to the PD Office if given the opportunity to intern there this summer.

I will contact you in a couple of weeks to confirm that you received this letter and my enclosed resume. Before then, if you have questions regarding my qualifications, please contact me at (805) 123-4567 or at lmm@wustl.edu. Thank you in advance for your consideration. I look forward to speaking with you.

Sincerely,

Laura M. Mackey
Laura M. Mackey
Encl.: resume

Notes:

1. Laura added a description of what was taught in her writing course, which may not be evident from the course title. She also added the specific skills in which she excelled that are directly relevant to the Employer's work.

2. Laura used sophisticated legal language when describing her job experience.

3. She included a statement that she would appreciate the opportunity to work with the Employer.

Sample 9.3

Before

Cover letter of Timothy Newstead (non-school connection).

Notes:

1. Timothy notes why he is attending law school. His goal is very specific and a bit narrow, given that he is a 1L. He might consider broadening it to show flexibility.

2. Timothy identifies and describes his public service work during law school. He notes that he is a member of a public service committee, but it is unclear if he is an active member.

3. The facts about Timothy's law school grades are unclear and, therefore, not persuasive. The facts about his undergraduate degree are evident from his resume and not persuasive when standing alone.

Timothy J. Newstead
7424 Buckingham Dr., Apt. 2D
St. Louis, MO 63105

January 12, 20XX

Ms. Jane Allen
101 Second Street, Suite 600
San Francisco, CA 94105

Dear Ms. Allen:

I am a first-year law student at Washington University in St. Louis School of Law. I am writing to express my interest in the internship position for the California Appellate Project this summer.

❶ My primary reason for choosing to attend law school was so that I could become a public defender. My desire to work in California has led me to apply for this position. **❷** I am currently a member of the Public Service Advisory Board at Washington University. PSAB is a student-led organization that allocates public service funds among student groups, facilitates educational events about public service careers, creates opportunities for public service within the law school and in the larger St. Louis community, and administers the Pro Bono Pledge. I am a member of the Public Service Committee, which organizes service projects to foster student involvement with the community. I believe that my involvement with this organization has strengthened my determination to pursue a career in public service.

❸ While I have not received my final grades for the first semester, I anticipate that I will have a solid GPA. I received high marks for papers in Legal Practice I and Criminal Law. I graduated from the University of Notre Dame in 2012 with a Bachelor of Science degree. I spent my last two years at Notre Dame volunteering as an after-school tutor for local youth and volunteering at a local hospital once a week. I believe that my commitment to service can be seen through these activities, as well as the year I spent living in Jamaica with the Passionist Volunteers International. I believe that spending the upcoming summer as an intern for the California Appellate Project would be an incredible opportunity and the first-step in realizing my goal of becoming a public defender.

I will be in Chicago during the weekend of February 6th for the Midwest Public Interest Law Career Conference. I would welcome the opportunity to meet with you during the conference to discuss the summer internship. Please feel free to contact me anytime at (314) 123-4567 or newsteadt@wustl.edu. Thank you in advance for your consideration.

Sincerely,

Timothy J. Newstead

Sample 9.4

After

Edited cover letter of Timothy Newstead (non-school connection).

Timothy J. Newstead
7424 Buckingham Dr., Apt. 2D
St. Louis, MO 63105

January 12, 20XX

Jane Allen, Esquire
California Appellate Project
101 Second Street, Suite 600
San Francisco, CA 94105

Dear Ms. Allen:

Sarah Volk, my friend and a former intern with the California Appellate Project (the "Appellate Project"), recommended that I apply for the 20XX summer internship. Sarah's enthusiasm for the work she did at the Appellate Project as an intern last summer inspired me to apply for an internship this summer. I am a first-year law student at Washington University in St. Louis School of Law. Like Sarah, I am committed to a career in public interest law, with an emphasis on criminal law. Please accept this letter and my enclosed resume as my application for a summer internship with the Appellate Project.

❶ My primary goal in attending law school is to work in criminal defense, perhaps as a public defender. I am currently a member of the Public Service Advisory Board at Washington University. PSAB is a student-led organization that allocates public service funds among student groups, facilitates educational events about public service careers, creates opportunities for public service within the law school and in the larger St. Louis community, and administers the Pro Bono Pledge. I am an active member of the Public Service Committee and have had the ❷ opportunity to organize service projects to foster student involvement with the St. Louis community. My involvement with this organization has strengthened my determination to pursue a career in public service.

❸ My commitment to public service predates law school. I spent my last two years at Notre Dame volunteering as an after-school tutor for local youth and weekly at a local hospital. I also spent a year after college living and working in Jamaica with the Passionist Volunteers International. My interest in criminal law stems from the challenges I observed many of my students enduring as their family members navigated the criminal justice system, often without consistent legal representation. I believe that spending this summer as an intern for the Appellate Project would be an incredible opportunity and the first step in realizing my goal of becoming a public defender.

I will be in Chicago during the weekend of February 6th for the Midwest Public Interest Law Career Conference, and welcome the opportunity to meet with you or one of your colleagues to discuss the Appellate Project and my qualifications for an internship with it. In the meantime, please feel free to contact me at (314) 123-4567 or newsteadt@wustl.edu. Thank you in advance for your consideration.

Sincerely,

Timothy J. Newstead

Encl.: Resume

Notes:

1. Timothy broadened his reasons for attending law school to include the work the Employer does.

2. He used the active voice when rephrasing the facts of his public service work, which conveys that he is an active participant.

3. Rather than including his law school grades, Timothy focused on his demonstrated long-term commitment to public service, a necessity for a public interest internship.

Sample 9.5

Before

Cover letter of Sally Nathan (weak or no connection).

Notes:

1. Sally combines two different work experiences in one sentence, which is difficult to follow.

2. Because Sally is applying to work with a private law firm in which client development is important, she should focus on her business development background more.

3. Sally notes that she is an elected representative of a law school organization, but without an explanation, the significance of that position is unclear.

Sally Nathan
123 Lake Drive
Kirkwood, MO 63122
(314) 123-4567
snathan@wustl.edu

Sara Cook
Director of Marketing & Law School Recruitment
800 Washington Avenue, Suite 2000
St. Louis, MO 63101

Dear Ms. Cook,

I am a first-year student at Washington University Law School and am writing to apply for a summer associate position with Smith Jones. I am confident my work experience combined with my professional qualities would make me an asset to your summer program. Having grown up in St. Louis, I would like to stay in the area after graduation to further explore my interest in commercial litigation.

① In addition to the practical skills I developed during my legal internship at an entrepreneurial and patent practice in Chicago, I gained extensive exposure to the Oil and Gas Industry while working for a global contractor management database company in Dallas. As the account manager for multiple Fortune 500 energy companies, I worked face-to-face with clients regarding their insurance, quality and regulatory information. I was active in business development by **②** organizing and leading prospect meetings, while continuing to provide exceptional customer service to strengthen current client relationships.

③ In my first year of law school, I have continued to strengthen my leadership experience as an elected representative of the Student Bar Association. I understand teamwork is the foundation to a positive work environment, and I believe my leadership skills would enhance the collegial culture of Smith Jones. An internship with Smith Jones would also provide me the opportunity to learn from skilled attorneys, allow me to hone important research, writing and advocacy skills, and provide a unique view of the Firm's various departments.

I would greatly appreciate the opportunity to meet with you to discuss the possibility of a summer internship position. Please feel free to contact me at (314) 123-4567, and I will follow up with a phone call within the next couple of weeks. Thank you in advance for your time and consideration.

Sincerely,

Sally Nathan

Sample 9.6

After

Edited cover letter of Sally Nathan (weak or no connection).

Sally Nathan
123 Lake Drive
Kirkwood, MO 63122
(314) 123-4567
snathan@wustl.edu

January 5, 20XX

Sara Cook, Esquire
Recruiting Chair
Smith Jones, LLP
800 Washington Avenue, Suite 2000
St. Louis, MO 63101

Dear Ms. Cook,

As a 1L student at Washington University Law School, I am reaching out to you as one of our alumni to get more information about your practice. Like you, I am from St. Louis and plan to practice law here. After working in Chicago and Dallas, it is nice to be back in St. Louis. In reviewing your firm's website, I noticed that Smith Jones has a large energy practice group. Given my experience in the oil and gas industry, I am interested in exploring energy law, and welcome the opportunity to speak with you or your colleagues about my background and the possibility of an internship for this coming summer.

① I am confident that my work experience combined with my professional qualities would make me an asset to your firm this coming summer. During my legal internship at an entrepreneurial and patent law firm in Chicago, I worked closely with senior attorneys and their clients on a variety of litigation related matters, and was responsible for reviewing filings and assisting in litigation proceedings. As the account manager for a Dallas-based global contractor, I worked with multiple Fortune 500 energy companies. In that role, I gained extensive exposure to the oil and gas industry working face-to-face with clients regarding their insurance, quality, and regulatory information. I was also active in business development by organizing and leading prospect **②** meetings while providing exceptional customer service to strengthen current client relationships. **③** I continue to bolster my professional leadership and business development skills in law school as an elected representative of the Student Bar Association ("SBA"). My participation in the SBA has allowed me to work with my fellow students as well as law school administrators to insure that 1Ls' interests are recognized and addressed. An internship with Smith Jones would allow me to use my work experience, provide me the opportunity to learn from skilled attorneys, and hone my research, writing, and advocacy skills.

I would greatly appreciate the opportunity to meet with you or one of your colleagues to discuss my qualifications for a summer internship. I will follow up with a phone call within the next couple of weeks to confirm that you received this letter and my enclosed resume. Before then, please let me know if you need additional information from me. Thank you in advance for your consideration.

Sincerely,

Sally Nathan

Sally Nathan

Encl.: resume

Notes:

1. Sally began the Facts with a sentence identifying the skills she brings to an Employer. She separated her two most significant work experiences, since she gained different skills from each one. Sally added specific facts about what she did at each experience.

2. By placing this sentence here, Sally created a connection between her business development experience, law school, and future legal work.

3. Sally added an explanation of her work with the SBA to show the Employer her experience working with different constituents, which is similar to working with parties and clients who have differing interests.

Checklist: Cover Letter — Facts

Facts:	Yes	No
Did you make a list of specific facts that you might include in this section of your letter?		
Did you make a list of phrases that describe you and that include facts?		
If you read these sentences out loud, do they sound conversational?		
Did you include your goals related to the reason you want to work with the Employer?		
Do the Facts lead into the reasons why you are a good fit for the Employer?		
Proofing:		
Is the font for the Facts consistent with your resume and the rest of your letter?		
Is the Facts paragraph formatted consistently with the rest of your letter (i.e., indented the same number of spaces, spacing between lines)?		
Are there any proofing errors (misspelled words, including names, incorrect punctuation, etc.)?		

Chapter 10

Discussion/Argument: Why Are You a Good Fit for Our Organization?

Purpose of Section

This section is similar to the "Summary of Argument" in a brief: in it, you make a case for why an Employer should interview and ultimately hire you. Think of two or three specific reasons why you are the best person for the job and make the argument. If you can "prove" those reasons using the Facts section, this section will be even more persuasive.

Step-by-Step Guide

Similar to a summary of argument, think of a theme as to why you are a good fit for the Employer's organization and make your argument using facts to "prove" your theme. Themes that resonate with Employers focus on proving that you: 1) have the intellectual ability to do the work; 2) have done related or similar work; and 3) possess the professional skills necessary to be both successful in the Employer's legal practice and part of the next generation of leaders. Sound familiar? It should. These are the same themes conveyed in your resume. The order in which you discuss them depends on you — your academic background, and your work and leadership experiences.

Intellectual Ability

For intelligence, focus on academics and highlight your research and writing prowess, either through a particular sophisticated project, excellent grades in those subjects, or significant work experience that required those skills. Focus on skills acquired in law school rather than those learned in undergraduate school. Review your resume and list facts that prove your research and writing abilities. One strategy, when drafting this paragraph, is to first verbally tell someone those facts and then put those words into writing.

Transferable Skills

With respect to transferable skills, emphasize academic or work experience that relates to that Employer. If you are pursuing an opportunity with a patent law firm, emphasize your engineering background. When applying to a legal services office, emphasize your commitment to public service as evidenced by specific work experience. With public interest organizations, a history of commitment to the field is expected.

Professional and Leadership Skills

Use community engagement experiences as proof that you possess these skills. Community engagement means everything from fundraising for non-profits to volunteering with Big Brother/Big Sister or a similar organization. Professional and leadership skills involve working as a team with people who have more authority than you (administrators and supervisors) and those for whom you are an authority (junior colleagues). Convey that you have the proven ability to relate to, and be comfortable with, a variety of people. Use specific examples of your accomplishments, not just the word "Leadership." Examples of such accomplishments are appointed or elected positions to a university honor council, or a university-wide or community group. The legal profession, even for solo practitioners, is one in which attorneys constantly interact with others — clients, court personnel, community groups, other attorneys, etc. Therefore, it is critical that you identify examples of your success in such interactions.

Chapter 10

Sample Cover Letters

Discussion/Argument

Sample 10.1

Before

Cover letter of Denise Hollander (school connection).

Notes:

1. Denise identifies "work ethic" and "enthusiasm" as themes or reasons why she would be a good fit for this Employer.

2. She focuses on academic achievement, which was not included as one of her themes, and is therefore confusing.

3. Denise focuses on her leadership skills as another reason why she would be a good fit for this Employer, but without mentioning "leadership skills" earlier, it will be harder for an Employer to follow her argument.

DENISE ALYSSA HOLLANDER
1234 West Pine Blvd #10L • St. Louis, MO 63108
dahollander@wustl.edu
(941) 123-4567

January 14, 20XX

Ms. Marsha Dennis
Tucker Smith LLP
7000 Forsyth Blvd, Ste 1000
St. Louis, MO 63105

Dear Ms. Dennis:

I am a first-year Dean's Fellow at Washington University School of Law and am interested in a summer associate position with Tucker Smith in 20XX. I moved to St. Louis this past summer and am eager to gain experience in the St. Louis legal community, as I am planning to make St. Louis my permanent home. I am interested in exploring your firm's wide variety of practice areas, especially the firm's growing intellectual property practice area, and am excited by the opportunity to seek responsibility early on as an associate.

① I am confident that I have the work ethic and enthusiasm to be an asset to Tucker Smith this summer and beyond. In addition to maintaining a strong overall academic record, **②** ranking in the top XX% of my class, I have demonstrated my writing ability by earning the highest grade in my Legal Practice course, X.X. This builds on my prior research and writing experience obtained through journalistic training at the University of South Florida and as a media fellow for multiple organizations. Moreover, I developed leadership skills while serving **③** as vice president of USF Hillel, a Jewish campus organization, during which time I led executive student board meetings and worked in close partnership with the student president. I welcome the opportunity to apply and hone those skills while collaborating with team members at Tucker Smith.

Thank you for your time and consideration. I hope to have the opportunity to demonstrate why I am a great fit for your firm during an on-campus interview. In the meantime, please feel free to contact me at the telephone number or e-mail address listed above.

Sincerely,

Denise A. Hollander

Sample 10.2

After

Edited cover letter of Denise Hollander (school connection).

DENISE ALYSSA HOLLANDER
1234 West Pine Blvd #10L • St. Louis, MO 63108
dahollander@wustl.edu
(941) 123-4567

January 14, 20XX

Ms. Marsha Dennis
Tucker Smith LLP
7000 Forsyth Blvd
Suite 1000
St. Louis, MO 63105

Dear Ms. Dennis:

I recently spoke with John Holmes, one of your intellectual property attorneys, at the Employer Showcase hosted by Washington University School of Law ("Wash U Law"). I also had the opportunity to attend the 1L reception hosted by Tucker Smith in December. The collaborative and welcoming atmosphere of your firm was evident to me from both of those experiences. As a recent transplant to St. Louis, I am eager to make a connection in the St. Louis legal community with a firm like yours that has a varied, sophisticated practice as well as a reputation for community engagement. Please accept this letter and my attached resume as my application for a summer internship with Tucker Smith.

I am interested in exploring your firm's wide variety of practice areas, especially intellectual property, and am excited by the opportunity to seek responsibility early on as an associate. **I am confident that I have the research and writing skills, leadership skills,** ❶ **and enthusiasm to be an asset to Tucker Smith this summer and beyond.** In addition to maintaining a strong overall academic record, ranking in the top XX% of my class, I have ❷ demonstrated my writing ability in law school by earning the highest grade in my Legal Practice course, X.X. This builds on my prior research and writing experience obtained through journalistic training at the University of South Florida and as a media fellow for multiple organizations. Moreover, I developed leadership skills while serving in a variety of capacities at my undergraduate university and in the South Florida community. In addition to building a successful legal practice, it is important to me to be involved in my community. Tucker Smith's demonstrated commitment to the St. Louis community appeals ❸ to me.

I understand that Tucker Smith is participating in the on-campus interview program at Wash U Law and I welcome the opportunity to meet with you or one of your colleagues. In the meantime, please contact me if there is any other information you need from me at this time.

Sincerely,

Denise Hollander

Denise Hollander

Encl.: resume

Notes:

1. Denise revised her themes, or reasons why she would be an asset to the Employer, to be "research and writing skills, leadership skills, and enthusiasm." All of these themes are critical to the Employer with whom Denise is applying for an internship.

2. She included specific facts that prove each theme in the same order as her themes.

3. Denise related her abilities and goals to the Employer's practice and its commitment to community engagement.

Sample 10.3

Before

Cover letter of Carrie Yu (non-school connection).

Notes:

1. Carrie provides examples of facts that relate to the reasons why she would be a good fit for the Employer, but she does not include a statement identifying her theme. She gives an example of her significant research and writing experience from her undergraduate school, but it would be more persuasive to add such experience from law school.

2. Carrie includes her work as a paralegal with a large law firm but does not include her specific duties or projects.

Carrie S. Yu
12 South Kingshighway Blvd., Apt. 12S
St. Louis, MO 63108
(703) 123-4567
carriesyu@wustl.edu

December 18, 20XX

Valerie Rogers
Senior Manager, Recruiting & Retention
Davis Smith P.C.
1234 Main Street
Indianapolis, IN 46204

Dear Ms. Rogers,

I am a first-year student at Washington University School of Law and I hope to be considered for a 1L Summer Associate position at the New York Office of Davis Smith. I worked in New York for two years before attending law school and hope to return to the area after graduation. I am specifically interested in working for Davis Smith because I admire the firm's impressive labor and employment practice. Furthermore, having chatted extensively with Sarah Jones at the National Asian Pacific American Bar Association Conference in New Orleans this November, I truly admire Davis Smith's dedication to diversity.

I believe I am the ideal candidate for this position for a number of reasons. Having worked as a **①** Research Assistant for both the Government and Psychology Departments at Georgetown as well as the Psychology Department at University College London, I have the research and writing skills necessary to be a successful associate. Furthermore, having worked as a Litigation **②** Paralegal at Paul Weiss for the two years prior to law school, I know that my attention to detail, perfectionist personality, and strong work ethic are characteristics that will allow me to succeed in the fast paced environment of Davis Smith.

I plan to be in New York during the first week of January and I am able to take a quick train up to the city at any time between now and January 8th when I return to St. Louis for school. I would greatly appreciate the opportunity to meet with someone in the New York Office to discuss how I can be an asset to Davis Smith. I look forward to hearing from you.

Sincerely,

Carrie S. Yu

Sample 10.4

After

Edited cover letter of Carrie Yu (non-school connection).

Carrie S. Yu
12 South Kingshighway Blvd., Apt. 12S
St. Louis, MO 63108
(703) 123-4567
carriesyu@wustl.edu

December 18, 20XX

Ms. Valerie Rogers
Senior Manager, Recruiting & Retention
Davis Smith P.C.
1234 Main Street
Indianapolis, IN 46204

RE: <u>Davis Smith New York Internship</u>

Dear Ms. Rogers,

I met Sarah Jones from your firm's New York office at the National Asian Pacific American Bar Association Conference in New Orleans this November, and she encouraged me to apply for a 1L summer associate position in the firm's New York office. Ms. Jones's enthusiasm for her labor and employment practice at Davis Smith, as well as the firm's demonstrated dedication to diversity, is very appealing to me. I worked in New York for two years before attending law school and plan to return to the area after graduation. I believe I am a very strong candidate for a summer associate position with your firm for a number of reasons.

(1) My research and writing skills, prior work experience, and ability to work in a fast-paced environment will be assets in this position. This fall, at the end of my first semester in law school, I received the highest grade in my Legal Practice (research and writing) section. This **(2)** grade was based on multiple research and writing assignments. For the two years prior to law **(3)** school, I worked as a Litigation Paralegal at a large, sophisticated New York City law firm. In that position, I supervised a team of paralegals in connection with a nationwide class-action lawsuit involving thousands of documents. I know that my attention to detail, perfectionist personality, and strong work ethic are characteristics that will allow me to succeed in the fast-paced environment of Davis Smith.

I will be in New York during the first week of January and welcome the opportunity to meet with you or your colleagues to discuss my qualifications for a summer associate position with Davis Smith. I will contact you in a couple of weeks to confirm that you received this letter and my enclosed resume. In the meantime, please let me know if you need additional information from me. Thank you in advance for your consideration.

Sincerely,

Carrie S. Yu
Carrie S. Yu

Encl.: resume

Notes:

1. Carrie specifically identified her themes as "research and writing skills, prior work experience, and ability to work in a fast-paced environment" — skills necessary for, and transferable to, the Employer.

2. Carrie used her law school academic achievements as examples of her research and writing skills rather than her undergraduate achievements.

3. She added her specific responsibilities as a paralegal, including the types of litigation matters she worked on.

Sample 10.5

Before

Cover letter of Stacy Stevens (weak or no connection).

Notes:

1. Stacy does not include all of her themes at the beginning of the argument section and rather generally incorporates them throughout her letter. This arrangement makes it difficult for the Employer to know immediately why she is a good fit.

2. Her leadership and other professional skills are lost in the middle of the paragraph. These are critical skills for this Employer and therefore should be prominent.

3. Stacy includes her law school academic achievement at the bottom of the long paragraph, which makes it seem less important.

Stacy A. Stevens

stacyastevens@wustl.edu
(504) 123-4567

January 25, 20XX

Rochelle Miller, Esquire
Carter Golden Legal Aid
123 N. Michigan Avenue
Chicago, IL 60642

Dear Ms. Miller:

I became interested in Carter Golden Legal Aid after PILI Executive Director Mathew Bruner's presentation in St. Louis this fall. As a first-year law student at Washington University School of Law, I was excited to learn of an opportunity to engage in public service throughout the city of Chicago. Having volunteered there during my sophomore year of college, I look forward to returning to the city to serve. I hope you will consider my application for an internship position this summer.

My desire for social change and public service was first fueled by research and discourse for a class called Poverty, Justice & Capabilities. The more we delved into the education gap, housing discrimination, miscarriages of justice, and the wealth disparity, the more I purposed to engage hands-on with those issues. I encountered Chicago's unique social issues in working with its homeless population at Inspiration Café and youth at the Boys and Girls Club. I coordinated with these organizations to tailor their initiatives to the growing needs of their community. I also generated solutions for balancing non-profit resources with the ability to address multiple levels of clients' well being. During my Criminology class visit to a state penitentiary, I worked with inmates to evaluate the benefits of education in prison and the necessity of comprehensive re-entry programs. Throughout my time with Teach for America, I battled the interplay between education, class, family structure, and race as I implemented individualized plans for students and engaged their families in fighting for their futures. In every country I visited on my mission trip, I addressed people's underlying needs through social initiatives, one-on-one meetings, and personalized support. As the Logistics Coordinator, I strengthened my leadership, communication, and time management skills. I coordinated with multiple parties, led large groups of diverse personalities, drove teams to complete time-sensitive projects, and balanced varied roles and responsibilities. My first semester of law school has integrated these experiences with legal concepts, analytical skills, and excellent writing abilities, having finished in the top fifteen percent of my Legal Practice I class last semester. My experiences combine with my legal education to equip me to be a valuable and immediate contributor to your office as a legal advocate for greater opportunities and stronger communities.

I am pursuing law school in order to contribute to the public interest sector, bridging my desire to provide justice for those who lack access to it and my belief that individuals can effect holistic change one life at a time. I am drawn to Carter Golden because of its vision to move beyond legal services and empower people and their communities. I consider your CLAIM program and Criminal Records division to be excellent examples of the multifaceted impact attorneys can have on men, women, children, and society as a whole.

I would welcome the opportunity to use my skills to advance your mission of bringing justice and mercy to those with the greatest need. It would be my pleasure to interview for an internship with you and I would be happy to provide any further information you may require.

Sincerely,

Stacy A. Stevens

Sample 10.6

After

Edited cover letter of Stacy Stevens (weak or no connection).

Stacy A. Stevens
stacyastevens@wustl.edu
(504) 123-4567

January 25, 20XX

Rochelle Miller, Esquire
Carter Golden Legal Aid
123 N. Michigan Avenue
Chicago, IL 60642

Dear Ms. Miller:

I became interested in Carter Golden Legal Aid after Executive Director Mathew Bruner's presentation in St. Louis this fall. As a first-year law student at Washington University School of Law, I am excited to learn of an opportunity to engage in public service in Chicago. I am pursuing law school because I have a desire to provide justice for those who lack access to it and I believe that individuals can affect change one life at a time. I am drawn to Carter Golden because of its vision to empower people and their communities. Your CLAIM program and Criminal Records division are excellent examples of the multifaceted impact attorneys can have on men, women, children, and society as a whole. Please consider this letter and my enclosed resume as my application for an internship position this summer.

① My passion for social justice, and my work experience and academic achievements in law school, will allow me to be a valuable and immediate contributor to your office as a legal advocate. My desire for social change and public service was first fueled by research and discourse for a class called Poverty, Justice & Capabilities. That course inspired my commitment to finding a way to engage hands-on with issues of the education gap, housing discrimination, miscarriages of justice, and wealth disparity. I was fortunate to work **②** with Chicago's homeless population at Inspiration Café and youth at the Boys and Girls Club. As part of my work, I generated solutions for stretching non-profit resources to address multiple levels of clients' wellbeing. Throughout my time with Teach for America, I battled the interplay between education, class, family structure, and race as I implemented individualized plans for students and engaged their families in fighting for students' futures. As the Logistics Coordinator for a yearlong mission trip, I strengthened my leadership, communication, and time management skills. I coordinated with multiple parties, led large groups of diverse personalities, drove teams to complete time-sensitive projects, and balanced varied roles and responsibilities.

In addition to my passion for social justice, I understand the need for working with the system to effect change. In law school, I am integrating my real world experiences with legal concepts, analytical skills, and **③** legal training. I was proud to score in the top fifteen percent in Legal Practice (legal writing) last semester. This past semester, I was also honored to be a Finalist in the Client Counseling Competition for 1Ls.

I welcome the opportunity to use my skills and growing legal knowledge to advance your mission of bringing justice and mercy to those with the greatest need. It would be my pleasure to interview for an internship with you and I would be happy to provide any further information you may require. I will contact you in a few weeks to confirm that you received this letter and my enclosed resume and to see if there is any other information you need from me to consider my application for an internship with Carter Golden.

Sincerely,

Stacy A. Stevens
Stacy A. Stevens

Encl.: resume

Notes:

1. Stacy began the Argument section with her themes: "passion for social justice, work experience, and academic achievements in law school." The Employer now has a roadmap to follow her argument.

2. She included specific examples of each theme as a reason for why she is a good fit for the Employer.

3. Stacy separated out her academic achievements in law school, which emphasizes them.

Checklist: Cover Letter — Discussion/Argument

Discussion/Argument:	Yes	No
Did you identify two or three themes or general reasons why you are a good fit for the Employer?		
Intellectual Ability:		
Did you include achievements related to legal research and writing in law school?		
Did you include specific examples of your achievements (i.e., a grade on a specific project, an award, etc.)?		
Transferable Skills:		
Did you include relevant academic or work experience and relate it to the Employer's work?		
Did you include specific examples of such academic or work experience?		
Professional and Leadership Skills:		
Did you include university or community engagement experiences that highlight your professional skills and leadership ability?		
Did you include your specific duties and not just the name of a title you held as a leader?		
Did you include examples of circumstances in which you worked with supervisors?		
Did you include examples of circumstances in which you supervised others?		
Did you include examples of leadership awards or honors?		
Proofing:		
Is the font for the Discussion/Argument consistent with your resume and the rest of your letter?		
Is this section formatted consistently with the rest of your letter?		
Are there any proofing errors (misspelled words, incorrect punctuation, etc.)?		

Chapter 11

Closing: How Do I End My Letter and What Is the Next Step?

Purpose of Section

The Closing of your letter is different than the conclusion of a legal memo or brief. It is not a summary of your letter; rather, the Closing is your opportunity to re-establish the relationship you established in the Introduction and to convey your next step. It lets you "keep the ball in your court" for a little while longer.

Step-by-Step Guide

First, thank an Employer for considering your application. Second, reiterate your enthusiasm for that Employer's practice. If you did not include a statement in the Introduction noting that your resume was enclosed, do so in the Closing. Third, identify the next step you will take in pursuit of an opportunity to work with that Employer. This could be: 1) calling or sending an email to confirm receipt of your letter and other application materials; 2) letting an Employer know you will be in a particular city and available to meet; or 3) noting that you hope to have the opportunity to meet that Employer in person. Fourth, include a statement with your contact information, letting an Employer know that if they have questions before you follow up, to please contact you. You can end the Closing where you began, with a short thank-you for considering your application.

Unless asked to do so, do not say that you will call to schedule a time to meet or interview. As hard as it is, you will need to wait to see if an Employer suggests a meeting or interview. Please keep in mind that hiring students is second to an Employer's day-to-day legal practice and it may take time to get back to you. If you noted your next step, the good news is that you have a reason to contact an Employer again. Remember to follow through; if you stated that you would confirm receipt of your letter in two weeks, call or send that email in two weeks. Following through is an example of your professional skills.

Signature and Enclosures

The last part of the Closing includes your signature. Unless you know an Employer personally and it would seem odd to sign a letter with your full name, sign your letter with the full name you used on your resume. Type your name and leave a space above it for your signature.

If enclosing your resume and other materials, include an "Encl.:" or "Encls.:," as appropriate, with the names of the documents in the lower left hand margin. If you identified a personal contact in the first sentence of your letter, consider copying that contact with a "cc." If you do copy that person, be sure to send him or her an actual copy of everything you send the addressee. Here is what this would look like:

Encl: resume
cc: Susan Jones, Esquire

Sending Your Cover Letter via Email

If sending your letter via email, send it as a PDF so that it looks like a real letter. (Letters sent in the body of email often look different than they do on paper.) To do this, attach your letter to your email as a separate document. You may have to scan your signed letter or use an electronic signature. To use an electronic signature, scan your signature and save it as an image file — usually as a jpeg or gif file. Once you have saved your signature in this manner, you can insert it in any document. You can have several signatures saved, including your full, legal name or just your first name, to use as needed.

When sending your cover letter via email, put the name of your contact — the person who referred you — in the "Re" or "Subject" line. Something like "Referred by Susan Jones" will be fine. Do not put "Internship Application" or "Job Application" in the subject line of your email unless required for a particular application. A recipient will be much more likely to read your email, and therefore your resume and cover letter, if you include your contact's name as the subject.

Additional Tips for International Students

It may be inappropriate in certain cultures to suggest the next step after sending a cover letter, but not in the U.S. It is common practice in the U.S. to follow up with an Employer after sending a cover letter rather than to wait to hear back. Suggest a "next step" consistent with the guidelines in this chapter and that will be appropriate.

Chapter 11

Sample Cover Letters

Closing

Sample 11.1

Before

Cover letter of Matthew Novack (school connection).

Notes:

1. Matthew includes his contact info but does not identify the next step he will take. He thanks the Employer for considering his application.

2. Matthew needs to add his signature. If he sends the cover letter via email, his signature will be an image file.

3. Matthew does not indicate whether he included his resume or other documents.

Matthew T. Novack
7025 Forsyth Dr.
St. Louis, MO 63105
(845) 123-4567
mtnovack@wustl.edu

January 24, 20XX

Mr. Benjamin Cruse
Commodity Futures Trading Commission
140 Broadway
New York, NY 10005

Dear Mr. Cruse,

I am a first year law student at Washington University in St. Louis writing to apply for the Commodity Futures Trading Commission's 20XX Summer Internship Program.

I am pursuing a career in securities litigation and white collar criminal prosecution. A position as a summer intern at the CFTC will provide me with an unparalleled opportunity to pursue these interests and apply my own corporate experience in a way that will contribute substantively to the Commission's efforts.

During my first semester of law school, I excelled in all of my classes and I received the highest grade in my torts class of approximately 80 students. Overall, my GPA places me on the Dean's List and in the top XX% of my grade. My success this semester is a testament to the ambition I will bring to the CFTC.

Prior to law school I worked as a market research analyst for a business information firm called Avention, where I researched corporate information technology trends and immersed myself in financial statements and SEC filings using the SEC's EDGAR database. I compiled reports on information technology and corporate expenditures in a variety of industries, using U.S. Census Bureau economic data and American FactFinder to extrapolate trends and identify growth areas. My technical understanding of corporate underpinnings is a great asset to any securities litigator or white collar prosecutor, and I know it will serve me well at the CFTC.

1 Please feel free to contact me at (845) 123-4567 or mtnovack@wustl.edu if you have any questions. Thank you in advance for your time and consideration. I look forward to hearing from you

Sincerely,

2

Matthew T. Novack
3

Sample 11.2

After

Edited cover letter of Matthew Novack (school connection).

Matthew T. Novack
(845) 123-4567
mtnovack@wustl.edu

<u>School Address</u>
7025 Forsyth Dr.
St. Louis, MO 63105

<u>Permanent Address</u>
16 Adams Court
Nanuet, NY 10954

January 24, 20XX

Benjamin Cruse, Esquire
Commodity Futures Trading Commission
140 Broadway
New York, NY 10005

RE: <u>20XX Summer Internship Program</u>

Dear Mr. Cruse,

Please accept the enclosed resume and personal statement as my application for the Commodity Futures Trading Commission's ("CFTC's") 20XX Summer Internship Program ("Internship"). I learned about the CFTC Internship at the Federal Government Career Fair held at my law school, Washington University in St. Louis–School of Law. I was intrigued by the opportunities that participants in the CFTC Internship have to participate in all phases of the CFTC's work. After law school, I plan to use my background in corporate work and psychology to pursue a career in securities litigation and white-collar criminal prosecution. If selected for the CFTC Internship, I welcome the opportunity to pursue my interests and to apply my corporate experience and expertise in securities research to contribute substantively to the CFTC's efforts.

Prior to law school, I worked as a market research analyst for a business information firm, where I researched corporate information technology trends and immersed myself in financial statements and SEC filings using the SEC's EDGAR database. I drafted reports on information technology and corporate expenditures in a variety of industries, using U.S. Census Bureau economic data and American FactFinder to extrapolate trends and identify growth areas. I believe that my technical understanding of corporate underpinnings and securities research experience will allow me to assist you and your colleagues at the CFTC this summer.

① I welcome the opportunity to speak with you or one of your colleagues about my interest in, and qualifications for, the CFTC Internship program. I will contact you in a couple of weeks to confirm receipt of my application materials. In the meantime, please contact me at (845) 123-4567 or mtnovack@wustl.edu if you have any questions. Thank you in advance for your time and consideration.

Sincerely,

② *Matthew T. Novack*
Matthew T. Novack

③ Encls.: Resume
            Statement of Interest

Notes:

1. Matthew noted his interest in speaking with the Employer and identified his next step: he will contact the addressee to make sure he received this letter and other application materials.

2. Matthew included his signature as an image file.

3. He noted that his resume and statement of interest are included with his letter.

Sample 11.3

Before

Cover letter of Carrie Yu (non-school connection).

Notes:

1. Carrie notes when she will be in New York but provides too much detail regarding her travel plans. The Employer doesn't need this much information.

2. She lets the Employer know that she would like to meet to discuss an internship.

3. Carrie needs to add her signature.

4. Carrie needs to indicate if she is including her resume.

Carrie S. Yu
12 South Kingshighway Blvd., Apt. 12S
St. Louis, MO 63108
(703) 123-4567
carriesyu@wustl.edu

December 18, 20XX

Valerie Rogers
Senior Manager, Recruiting & Retention
Davis Smith P.C.
1234 Main Street
Indianapolis, IN 46204

Dear Ms. Rogers,

I am a first-year student at Washington University School of Law and I hope to be considered for a 1L Summer Associate position at the New York Office of Davis Smith. I worked in New York for two years before attending law school and hope to return to the area after graduation. I am specifically interested in working for Davis Smith because I admire the firm's impressive labor and employment practice. Furthermore, having chatted extensively with Sarah Jones at the National Asian Pacific American Bar Association Conference in New Orleans this November, I truly admire Davis Smith's dedication to diversity.

I believe I am the ideal candidate for this position for a number of reasons. Having worked as a Research Assistant for both the Government and Psychology Departments at Georgetown as well as the Psychology Department at University College London, I have the research and writing skills necessary to be a successful associate. Furthermore, having worked as a Litigation Paralegal at Paul Weiss for the two years prior to law school, I know that my attention to detail, perfectionist personality, and strong work ethic are characteristics that will allow me to succeed in the fast paced environment of Davis Smith.

① I plan to be in New York during the first week of January and I am able to take a quick train up to the city at any time between now and January 8th when I return to St. Louis for school. I would ② greatly appreciate the opportunity to meet with someone in the New York Office to discuss how I can be an asset to Davis Smith. I look forward to hearing from you.

Sincerely,
③
Carrie S. Yu

④

Sample 11.4

After

Edited cover letter of Carrie Yu (non-school connection).

Carrie S. Yu
12 South Kingshighway Blvd., Apt. 12S
St. Louis, MO 63108
(703) 123-4567
carriesyu@wustl.edu

December 18, 20XX

Ms. Valerie Rogers
Senior Manager, Recruiting & Retention
Davis Smith P.C.
1234 Main Street
Indianapolis, IN 46204

RE: <u>Davis Smith New York Internship</u>

Dear Ms. Rogers,

I met Sarah Jones from your firm's New York office at the National Asian Pacific American Bar Association Conference in New Orleans this November, and she encouraged me to apply for a 1L summer associate position in the firm's New York office. Ms. Jones's enthusiasm for her labor and employment practice at Davis Smith, as well as the firm's demonstrated dedication to diversity, is very appealing to me. I worked in New York for two years before attending law school and plan to return to the area after graduation. I believe I am a very strong candidate for a summer associate position with your firm for a number of reasons.

My research and writing skills, prior work experience, and ability to work in a fast-paced environment will be assets in this position. This fall, at the end of my first semester in law school, I received the highest grade in my Legal Practice (research and writing) section. This grade was based on multiple research and writing assignments. For the two years prior to law school, I worked as a Litigation Paralegal at a large, sophisticated New York City law firm. In that position, I supervised a team of paralegals in connection with a nationwide class-action lawsuit involving thousands of documents. I know that my attention to detail, perfectionist personality, and strong work ethic are characteristics that will allow me to succeed in the fast-paced environment of Davis Smith.

(1) I will be in New York during the first week of January and welcome the opportunity to meet with you or your colleagues to discuss my qualifications for a summer associate position with Davis Smith. I will contact you in a couple of weeks to confirm that you received this letter and my **(2)** enclosed resume. In the meantime, please let me know if you need additional information from me. Thank you in advance for your consideration.

Sincerely,

(3) *Carrie S. Yu*
Carrie S. Yu

(4) Encl.: resume

Notes:

1. Carrie noted when she will be in New York and welcomed the opportunity to meet with the Employer during that time.

2. She included the next step she will take to follow through with the Employer. She thanked the Employer for considering her application.

3. Carrie added her signature.

4. Carrie included the appropriate notation indicating that she enclosed her resume.

Sample 11.5

Before

Cover letter of Frank Douglas (weak or no connection).

Notes:

1. Frank does not indicate the next step he will take to follow through with the Employer. He does include a brief thank-you.

2. Frank needs to add his signature.

3. Frank needs to add a notation that he is enclosing his resume.

Dear Mr. Winston,

I am a first-year student at Washington University School of Law, and I am writing to express my interest in the 1L summer internship offered by the EPA's Philadelphia office.
My main goal in applying to law school was to eventually find a job in the field of environmental law. My interest in environmental issues began in college, where I took classes on the environmental consequences of globalization, the philosophical problems of climate change, and the rational choice theory behind international negotiations on environmental agreements. Since my undergraduate years, my desire to work in the environmental field has only grown stronger. As a first-year law student I have not yet had the opportunity to take any classes in environmental law, but I have dedicated my personal time to working with Washington University's Energy and Environmental Law Society (EELS) as an elected board member. In that capacity, I've both learned more about climate change and broadened the scope of my interest to include other environmental problems. The state of the environment strikes me as one of the most critical issues facing the world right now, and I believe that spending my career working on environmental issues would bring me more professional fulfillment than working in any other practice area. I believe that this position at the EPA presents an incredible opportunity to learn about the type of work that environmental lawyers do.

In my first semester of law school, I performed especially well in Contracts and Legal Research. I believe that the attention to detail and the precise thinking required for Contracts classes would be a useful asset to a 1L intern. Furthermore, if I am asked to do any research, the skills I have learned in my Legal Research class will surely help me to be a more successful intern. I am a fast learner, and will work hard to pick up any skills necessary to be useful to your office as an intern. I feel that with this range of qualities I have the ability to be a productive member of your office despite my lack of professional legal experience.

1 If you have any questions, please feel free to contact me at (609) 123-4567 or fddouglas@wustl.edu. Thank you for your time and consideration.

Sincerely,

2

Frank D. Douglas

3

Sample 11.6

After

Edited cover letter of Frank Douglas (weak or no connection).

Frank D. Douglas

1234 Lindell Blvd., Apt. W-504
St. Louis, MO 63108

(609) 123-4567
fddouglas@wustl.edu

January 25, 20XX

Mr. Thomas Winston
U.S. Environmental Protection Agency
Region III (3RC00)
1650 Arch Street
Philadelphia, PA 19103-2029

Dear Mr. Winston,

As a first-year student at Washington University School of Law ("Law School"), I am writing to express my interest in the Legal Internship ("Internship") at the Environmental Protection Agency ("EPA") office in Philadelphia. Past participants and fellow law students, Roseanne Brown and John Caruthers, recommended that I apply.

My lifelong interest in environmental issues, research skills, and ability to communicate would make me an effective EPA intern. My interest in the environment, particularly climate change, is one of the reasons I decided to attend law school. As an attorney, I want to use my passion and legal knowledge to impact policies that will benefit future generations. As an undergraduate, I studied the environmental consequences of globalization, philosophical problems of climate change, and rational choice theory behind international environmental agreements. While I have not had the opportunity as a first-year law student to take environmental law classes, I have dedicated my personal time to working with the Law School's Energy and Environmental Law Society as an elected board member. In that capacity, I have learned more about climate change and broadened the scope of my interest in environmental issues. I earned one of my highest grades this past semester in legal research, and am anxious to put that skill into practice in the environmental area. Prior to law school I taught English as a Second Language as part of a ministry program. As a teacher, I learned to communicate effectively with supervisors and students. My passion for the environment, research ability and communication skills would be an asset to the EPA.

❶ I will be in the Philadelphia area in March and welcome the opportunity to meet with you or one of your colleagues then to learn more about the Internship and share my thoughts on why I would be an asset to the program. I will contact you in a few weeks to confirm that you received ❷ this letter and my enclosed resume and to see if there is a convenient time for us to meet in March. In the meantime, if you have any questions, please contact me. Thank you for your consideration.

Sincerely,

❸ *Frank D. Douglas*
Frank D. Douglas

❹ Encl.: Resume

Notes:

1. Frank noted when he will be in Philadelphia, the Employer's location, and said that he welcomed the opportunity to meet with the Employer.

2. He indicated the next step he will take to confirm receipt of his letter and resume, and to see if there is a convenient time to meet.

3. Frank included his signature as an image file.

4. He added the notation showing that his resume is included.

Checklist: Cover Letter — Closing

Closing:	Yes	No
Did you thank the Employer for considering your application?		
Did you convey your enthusiasm for the Employer's practice?		
Did you identify the next step you will take to follow up?		
Did you say that you would call or send an email to confirm receipt of your materials?		
If true, did you tell the Employer when you would be in the Employer's city to perhaps meet?		
Did you note that you hope to have the opportunity to meet with the Employer?		
Did you include your contact information if the Employer wants to contact you before you follow up?		
Signature and Enclosures:		
Did you use the same name on your resume for your signature?		
Did you include your signature above your typed name?		
If you enclosed your resume or other documents did you include an "Encl.:" or "Encls.:" with the name of the document or documents?		
If you identified a contact person in the first paragraph of your letter, did you add a "cc" with that person's name after the enclosures?		
If you added a contact's name, did you send that person a copy of everything you sent the addressee?		
Sending Your Letter via Email:		
Did you send your letter as a PDF?		
Did you include your scanned signature as an image file in your letter?		
Did you include your contact person's name in the subject matter line of your email?		
Proofing:		
Is the font for the Closing consistent with your resume and the rest of your letter?		
Is this section formatted consistently with the rest of your letter?		
Are there any proofing errors (misspelled words, incorrect punctuation, etc.)?		

Part III

Writing Samples, References and Recommendation Letters, and Networking

Chapter 12

Writing Samples:[1] What Is a Legal Writing Sample and How Do I Put One Together?

Purpose

The purpose of a writing sample is to provide an example of your writing to an Employer. It may also be used to as a screening tool to determine whether to interview you or offer you a position. Either way, writing samples are used to distinguish applicants and are critical to your job search, because they send a message about you. Employers know that you have complete control over what you submit; therefore, they assume that your writing sample represents your best work.

What Kind of Document Should I Submit as a Writing Sample?

Employers are looking for someone to research the law, analyze it, and communicate that analysis in writing. Your writing sample should showcase these three skills, and look like something that was produced in a legal organization. Most 1L students use an open research project from first or second semester, such as a memorandum ("memo") or a brief. A memo requires an objective analysis and explanation of the law, a typical project for newer attorneys; a brief showcases your persuasive writing skills. It is helpful to have both an objective and a persuasive writing sample when going into your 2L year.

If you are a 2L or 3L student and you want to use a project from a summer internship, choose something that showcases the three critical skills of research, analysis, and writing, and that was not edited by anyone other than you. In addition, ask permission from your legal organization to use that project as a writing sample. After obtaining permission, excise out all identifying information.

Should I Always Send a Writing Sample?

If a writing sample is required for an application, you must send one. If it is not required, I recommend that you wait to send it until you are asked to do so. I say this for a couple of reasons. First,

---

1. This chapter is based on, and draws from, a handout developed by Professor Ann Davis Shields, Professor of Practice and Director of Pretrial Advocacy at Washington University School of Law in St. Louis. I am grateful for her generosity in allowing me to include this information for you.

if you wait until asked, this gives you another opportunity to contact an Employer, and the more times you contact an Employer, the more you stay "top-of-mind." Second, it is too easy to have a mistake in a writing sample and you do not want to give the Employer any reason to pass you over for an internship. In general, Employers ask for writing samples after applicants make the initial cut, such as following a screening interview.

Step-by-Step Guide

Length

In general, your writing sample should be between 5–10 pages. This means that you may not be able to use your entire memo or brief. Some or all of the discussion of a memo, or the argument section of a brief, should be included, as they are the most important sections of those documents. Your 1L memo or brief may be 15 pages or longer. To turn that into a 5–10 page writing sample (while keeping the font legible), do the following:

1) Copy the memo/brief into a new document and make the font 12-point Times New Roman. A font smaller than 12-point is difficult to read. If necessary, change the spacing to 1½ lines rather than double-spaced.

2) Keep all of the headings, including the general section headings. However, for all sections except for the Discussion and Argument, delete the text. Under the headings without text, write the words "[Intentionally Deleted]." This shows an Employer that you know there is a section at that place in the document, but you deleted it for brevity.

3) If there are multiple issues in your memo/brief, or if it is longer than 10 pages, decide which issues are examples of your best work. Use those in your writing sample.

4) Delete the sections of your memo/brief addressing issues you will not include in your writing sample, but keep the point headings. Under those headings, add the words "[Intentionally Deleted]" where the text was deleted. If you delete certain sections, remember to revise the introduction, summary, or conclusion as necessary.

5) Once your writing sample is within the 5–10 page range, put it into context for the Employer by adding a note on the first page, explaining the project. In the note, identify the source of the writing sample and the omitted sections. Briefly describe relevant client facts that gave rise to the legal issues addressed in your writing sample.

6) Create a header on the first page identifying your name and page number.

7) Proof, proof, and proof again. Eliminate all Bluebook, grammatical, and proofing errors. Attention to detail is a critical skill for an attorney and your writing sample is one way an Employer gauges whether you possess it.

8) Make your writing sample visually appealing. Check that all margins are even, headings are centered as necessary, the print is clear and even, and, if it is in hard copy, that there are no printer smudge marks.

9) As a final step, ask a very careful reader—someone you trust—to read your writing sample closely for errors you may have missed. When your reader tells you there are no errors, you are ready to submit your writing sample to an Employer.

The following pages are examples of the format discussed above for writing samples based on: 1) a memo; and 2) a brief.

Format for Writing Sample Using a Memorandum

Jo Ellen D. Lewis – page 1 of 10
Writing Sample
(insert heading on all pages)

NOTE: This writing sample is based on a Legal Writing I assignment. I represented the defendant/landlord, Redman Realty, in connection with a potential lawsuit threatened by one of its tenants, Ms. Jones. Ms. Jones was assaulted by a third party in the common area of a building owned by Redman Realty. The purpose of this assignment was to research and analyze ... For purposes of this writing sample, I deleted the Questions Presented, Short Answers, and Statement of Facts ... For brevity, I deleted Issues I and II, which addressed ...

****

MEMORANDUM

TO: Senior Attorney
FROM: Jo Ellen D. Lewis
RE: Redman Realty – Potential Lawsuit by Tenant for Injuries Suffered from an Assault
DATE: November 15, 20XX

QUESTIONS PRESENTED
[Intentionally Deleted]

SHORT ANSWERS
[Intentionally Deleted]

STATEMENT OF FACTS
[Intentionally Deleted]

DISCUSSION

I.   Contractual Liability

[Intentionally Deleted]

II.   Statutory Liability

[Intentionally Deleted]

III.   Liability for Negligence

(Include all text.)

IV.   Potential Defenses

[Intentionally Deleted]

CONCLUSION

Format for Writing Sample Using an Appellate Court Brief

Jo Ellen D. Lewis – page 1 of 10
Writing Sample
(insert header on all pages)

NOTE: This writing sample is based on a Legal Writing II assignment. I represented the United States of America in an appeal filed by the defendant, Walter Hendley ("Defendant"), of the District Court's denial of Defendant's Motion to Suppress Identification Evidence. The issues on appeal were whether: I) the identification procedure used by the FBI was not impermissibly suggestive; and II) even if the identification procedure was impermissibly suggestive, Ms. Barnacle's identification was sufficiently reliable to outweigh any potential corrupting influence. For purposes of this writing sample, I have deleted the Table of Authorities and Issue II.

******

UNITED STATES COURT OF APPEALS

FOR THE NINTH CIRCUIT

UNITED STATES,
Appellee,

-against-

WALTER HENDLEY,
Appellant.

No. CR 15-025

BRIEF FOR APPELLEE

Attorney for Appellee
One Brookings Drive
St. Louis, Missouri 63130
(555) 123-4567

<u>TABLE OF CONTENTS</u>

TABLE OF AUTHORITIES

[Intentionally Deleted]

OPINION BELOW

(Include all text.)

ISSUES PRESENTED

I) (Include all text.)

II) [Intentionally Deleted]

STATEMENT OF THE CASE

(Include all text.)

SUMMARY OF ARGUMENT

(Include all text.)

ARGUMENT

(Include all text.)

I.   THE DISTRICT COURT'S DENIAL OF THE MOTION TO SUPPRESS
      SHOULD BE AFFIRMED BECAUSE THE IDENTIFICATION
      PROCEDURE USED BY THE FBI WAS NOT IMPERMISSIBLY
      SUGGESTIVE.

      (Include all text.)

   A. The Identification Procedure Used by the FBI Was Not Impermissibly
      Suggestive Because the Lineup Itself Was Proper.

      (Include all text.)

B. The Actions of the FBI Were Not Impermissibly Suggestive Because Those Actions Did Not Impermissibly Influence the Identification of the Defendant.

(Include all text.)

II.   [Intentionally Deleted]

CONCLUSION

(Include all text.)

Dated: April 6, 20XX   Respectfully submitted,

                                              Attorney for Appellee
                                              One Brookings Drive
                                              St. Louis, Missouri 63130
                                              (555) 123-4567

Chapter 13

References and Recommendation Letters: What Are They and How Do I Get One?

In addition to showing an Employer your great experience and credentials, you may be asked to provide references or letters of recommendation. Most students ask a professor in whose class they have done well or whom they know from a smaller class; this is a great place to start. Choose someone who knows you well enough to add something positive to your application that may not be obvious from your resume. For our purposes, assume that your reference or recommender will be a law professor.

References

A reference is someone who agrees to be "on call" if an Employer chooses to reach out to that person. Your reference may or may not be called to vouch for you; however, if an Employer asks for a reference, expect that he or she will be called. This is true for non-profit, for-profit, and government Employers. Ask your professor, either in person or via email, if he or she is willing to serve as a reference. Provide your current resume and ask whether he or she needs anything else from you. Also, tell your professor why you are asking him or her to serve as a reference; you may have a particular interest in that professor's field of expertise, or did particularly well in his or her class, or the professor knows you well given the small size of the class or its interactive nature. This gives the professor something to think about and relate to an Employer on your behalf. For example, students often ask me to be a reference because they enjoyed the small group work we did in class. This helps me focus on those students' leadership within the group and their demonstrated ability to work as members of a team when I speak with Employers.

The most important thing to remember when asking a professor to serve as a reference is to ask *before* you provide that professor's contact information to an Employer. Unfortunately, I, like many professors, have gotten calls from Employers about students who did not ask me to be a reference. Obviously, that is a problem. In these cases, the professors are not prepared, and the students look unprofessional for not checking with the reference first. Always let your references know when you provide their name to an Employer so that they can be ready for the call. Employers also like to hear that a student hoped they might call the reference, as this tells an Employer that the student really wants that job.

As you progress through law school and beyond, renew your reference request each year. Do not assume that because a professor agreed to serve as a reference for you one year that he or she will be a reference in future years. Finally, when you provide your professor's name and contact information, be sure to use your professor's official title. To get the title, check your school's website or ask your professor.

Recommendation Letters

Asking a professor to write a recommendation letter is very different from asking him or her to serve as a reference, because it requires your professor to do more than just respond to a call or an email. You, too, will need to do more than make the request and provide your resume. Approach the professor by email and provide your resume, along with information about the Employer for whom the letter is needed; this helps your professor tailor your letter for that Employer. Also give your professor your application materials, such as your statement of interest, application form, or cover letter. Some professors require a meeting to discuss the letter, and others ask students to draft the letter themselves. Be prepared for either circumstance. Even if you are not asked to draft the letter, it is enormously helpful to your professor if you can identify two or three things they could include in theirs. This shows initiative and provides you with the opportunity to make sure an Employer receives the information you want conveyed to them. Most professors will not use a student-drafted letter, but it is a good starting point.

In terms of timing, at least two weeks' notice to draft a letter is standard. Professors differ, however, in terms of timing, so be sure to ask your professor about his or her specific time requirement. Students do not always appreciate that professors write multiple drafts of recommendation letters before the final letter, just as you write multiple drafts of your memos and briefs. As you know, this process takes time. Also, most professors do not begin drafting a recommendation letter until they have received all of the student's materials. This means that you need to know the deadlines for your applications and plan accordingly.

Sometimes, students ask for a general recommendation letter, addressed to "Whom It May Concern." Most professors I know do not write such letters for one reason: it is not in a student's best interest. You need a recommendation letter that speaks to a particular Employer as to why you would be an asset to that Employer. A generic letter cannot do that.

Finally, thank your professor for writing a recommendation letter. A gift is totally unnecessary; a thank-you note is perfect. In addition, keep your professors informed as to the status of any position for which they served as a reference or recommender. We like to celebrate your successes and support you in times that are not successful. Keeping us posted on your progress is important for you, as it gives you another reason to stay connected in case you need something from us in the future.

Additional Tips for International Students

Consider asking a professor who can speak to your English language skills to serve as a reference or write a recommendation letter for you. Professors whom you have had for the following types of classes would be able to speak about such skills: legal research and writing; advocacy; a seminar or other writing class; and a practical skills/clinic course.

Chapter 14

Tips for Job Prospecting and Securing a Job: What Can I Do Now to Start Establishing My Professional Network?

One of the hardest facts to embrace is that your professional career is truly what you make of it. The greatest career services office or advisor can't give you a career that is satisfying to you; only you can do that. The best time to start putting that career into place is now. By using this book, you have already accomplished two crucial things to get your career rolling: you drafted a memorable resume and cover letter. Now it's time to start using them. In this chapter, we will talk about networking, using online systems to boost your career, and the importance of following up after you have networked and interviewed.

Networking in General

Some people have the "gift of gab." They can talk to anyone, anywhere, about anything. If you are one of those people, you are a natural at networking. If not, then you are like the many students who are less comfortable talking to people they do not know. In that case, what can you do to become a better networker?

First, put yourself in a position to network. Go to employer showcases hosted by your law school and events hosted by law firms or other legal organizations in your community. Reach out to organizations in your target city to make connections in that city. (We will talk more about that later in this chapter.) When you do attend networking events, watch people who are naturals; notice what they do and model their behavior. Networking is about making a connection with someone. To do this, make eye contact, shake the person's hand, and start the conversation by introducing yourself. You need to make a physical connection — eye contact and a handshake — before you make an intellectual one.

Second, ask a question. People, especially attorneys, love to talk and they love to talk about themselves. Get them talking by asking open-ended questions that encourage a longer response than a "yes" or "no." Some open-ended questions are:

- What is your area of legal practice?
- What made you decide to practice that kind of law?

- What do you like best about your practice?
- How has your area of practice changed since you began practicing?
- How do you think the practice of law, including your area of practice, will change in the next five years?
- If you could change anything about your practice, what would it be?
- What skills do successful attorneys in your practice area possess?

If you really want to get an attorney talking, ask him or her, "What is a typical day like for you?" 99% of the time you will get the answer, "There is no typical day." Then the attorney will begin telling you about different days. It may be difficult to cut the conversation off.

When it seems like the conversation may be ending, ask the attorney if you can contact him or her in the future with questions. Request the attorney's business card, but be aware that many attorneys only have v-cards (virtual cards) available electronically.

Finally, continue the conversation by sending an email telling your new contact how much you enjoyed meeting him or her, and that you hope to stay in contact as you develop your legal career. Attorneys, by nature, love to give advice, so most of them really enjoy mentoring law students. Take advantage of this fact as you stay in contact. Be careful, though, about asking for open-ended advice, as you do not want to "overwork" your contact. Rather, reach out when you have a specific question.

Networking Outside Your Law School

It is still possible to network even if you cannot do so in person. This is especially important if you want to practice in a target city that is not the one in which your law school is located. To do this, research bar associations and other legal associations in your target city. Most associations have free or inexpensive student memberships, and many offer mentorship programs. Get involved by volunteering to be on a committee or working on a program hosted by the association. Legal associations can be general (local bar associations) or by practice area (real estate or criminal defense). In terms of bar associations, explore community bar associations in addition to state or large city associations. For example, if Chicago is your target city, there are bar associations for Illinois, Chicago, and the Northern Suburban Bar Association. Join all three. It is sometimes easier to get to know people at the local association, but all are great sources for networking and jobs. An added plus of joining a bar association is that most have online job listings available to members.

In addition to bar associations, local associations that revolve around practice areas are great networking sources. This is because these associations have members in several disciplines. For example, national real estate professional associations have local chapters comprised of real estate attorneys and other real estate professionals, including architects and finance professionals. Such associations are important for your future business development. I know what you are thinking — "I just want a job; I am not thinking about getting business." But you will be thinking about the latter sooner than you think, and if you develop relationships with people who can send you business, it will be great for you personally and an Employer will be even more impressed with you.

Networking Inside Your Law School

Many students do not realize that a wealth of networking opportunities exist within your law school walls — your professors. If you are interested in a particular area of law, read your school's website and find out which faculty members have expertise in that area, and go see them. It doesn't matter if you have not had them for a class. Tell them you are interested in their area of practice. If you do not know which area of practice interests you, spend some time perusing your law school's website and finding out what the faculty are doing. You are likely to read about an article, project, or conference that some faculty member is involved with and that interests you. It is not necessary to commit to a particular area of law at this point; all you need is an interest. Law school is a time to explore potential interests and there is no better way to see if something interests you than trying it out.

You can also ask the professor if he or she needs a research assistant. When you are a research assistant, you gain two things: expertise in a practice area and, hopefully, a mentor for life. Most professors teach for two reasons: they love to study the law and they love to mentor students. Many 1Ls choose to be a research assistant the summer before 2L year, as it is a chance to not only get paid, but to work on their research and writing skills and get to know a faculty member who can be a reference in the future. Some professors will post notices that they are looking for a research assistant and others will not. It doesn't matter; you are welcome to ask a professor about a research assistantship whether or not there is a posting. When seeking a research assistantship, approach it as you would any other job search. Send an email (cover letter) to a professor or stop by his or her office to tell the professor that you are interested in doing research with him or her and that you would like to submit an application. Try to make an appointment for a lengthier conversation (an interview) rather than just talking with the professor when you stop by his or her office. Bring your resume with you or send it when you ask for an appointment. If you do stop by the professor's office in person, it is not necessary to wear business formal, but business casual will make a nice impression.

Another way to network in your school is to get involved with student associations, either law school-based or university-wide. An active role in an association or on a committee gives you the opportunity to meet other law students — your future colleagues — and attorneys. The emphasis is on "active role," as just being a member is not as valuable to you. Most law school student associations are actively engaged with attorneys and other professionals in the community who have similar interests. If you are the person who invites those attorneys and professionals to speak to your group, you have a great opportunity to network.

Networking via LinkedIn

It has been said that LinkedIn is like Facebook for attorneys. I don't know if this is true, as I do not recommend Facebook for future attorneys, but I do recommend that you set up a LinkedIn profile. There are many resources to help you set up a LinkedIn profile with search engine optimization (i.e., getting a lot of responses), but at this point in your career you only need a basic profile using standard LinkedIn sections. Start with a professional-looking picture. You do not need to hire a professional photographer, but do not use the picture your friend took of you at the beach even if it is a great one. Use a picture that makes you look like the future attorney you are. Include your legal education-in-process on your profile along with relevant work experiences. Use a shortened version of your resume as descriptors for the work experience section. In LinkedIn's "Summary" section, use the skill categories you identified on your resume to group your work experience (see Chapter 4). You can even upload your resume as a PDF. Your career development office may have suggestions for using LinkedIn. The National Association for Law Placement, Inc. (NALP) has information for law students on using LinkedIn and LinkedIn also offers tips for students on using the site.

One of the most important features of LinkedIn is the ability to network by making connections. You can start networking by sending a request to be connected with your professors and your class-mates. When you work during the summer, be sure to connect with your colleagues.

LinkedIn can be a source of jobs, as well. It is possible to search for legal internships by area of practice and location under the "Jobs" tab. Even if you end up with only one lead, it is worth the few minutes it takes to search the site.

Like your resume, update your LinkedIn profile on a regular basis. As you gain more legal experi-ence and obtain new skills, make sure that your LinkedIn profile reflects that new information.

Following Up

There are several circumstances in which you will want to follow up with an attorney. The most obvious time to follow up is after an interview. Students routinely ask me if they should send a thank-you letter after an interview. My standard response is, "Only if you want the job."

However, you have the opportunity to follow up with an attorney even before an interview. If you met an attorney at a networking event, it would be a great idea to send an email letting the attorney know how much you enjoyed meeting him or her and that you hope to have an opportunity to speak again in the future. If that attorney's legal organization will be interviewing at your law school, let him or her know that you would appreciate the opportunity to interview with the firm during their on-campus visit.

If you are fortunate enough to get a screening interview with a legal organization, send a follow-up email to the interviewer thanking him or her for their time. Mention one thing you discussed during the interview and use that as a way to convey your continued interest in the organization and your de-sire for an opportunity to meet other attorneys from the organization, i.e., a callback interview.

After a callback interview or an interview with several attorneys in a legal organization, send a thank-you note. An email is fine. If the legal organization has a recruiting coordinator who orga-nized your interview, you can either send an email to that coordinator or separate emails to each attorney who interviewed you. If you send an email to the recruiting coordinator, highlight some of your conversations with the attorneys and ask the coordinator to let them know how much you enjoyed meeting them. If you send a separate email to each attorney, highlight something from your conversation with that person. Whether you send one message or several, your thank-you note will end up in your file and will likely be mentioned when the legal organization is considering candi-dates for a position. This means it is important to be consistent with your message.

In addition to thanking an interviewer for his or her time, a follow-up email gives you an op-portunity to actually follow up on something from that interview. For example, when one of my 2L students interviewed with a tax attorney for a corporate position with a private law firm, he advised her to take a particular class in her 3L year. In her follow-up email, the student let the attorney know that she appreciated his advice and had in fact changed her schedule to add the class he recom-mended. That follow-up showed the attorney that she really wanted the position with that firm and was doing everything she could to obtain it. She did get the job, and the class he recommended did help in her practice. Sending follow-up and thank-you emails gives you some control over a process that can at times seem out of your control.

Appendices

Appendix A

Law Student Questionnaire

Law Student Questionnaire

Name: Year in Law School:

Educational Background:
Schools, degrees, majors, etc:

Honors, scholarships, and significant activities:

Work Experience:
Post-graduate experience (legal or non-legal):

Legal Practice Interests:
Geographic target area:

Public or private practice:

Legal practice areas of interest:

Goal for 1L summer:

Goal for 2L summer:

Future career goals:

2 years post law school graduation:

5 years post law school graduation:

Special skills and languages:

Personal interests: Fun autobiographical information to help your professors, career advisor, and an Employer get to know you quickly, such as hobbies, sports, accomplishments, favorite books, etc.:

Appendix B

Student Bios

Student Bios

0–1 Year Work Experience Between Undergraduate and Law School:

Frank Douglas: Frank's hometown is the New York City area. He would like to return to the Northeast to work in a large metropolitan city, including New York City, D.C., Philadelphia, or Boston. Frank graduated from a large research university in New York City with a B.A. in Economics and Philosophy. As a 1L, Frank does not have a preference between private and public practice; however, for his 1L summer, he would like to work at a public interest organization in New York City or D.C. that has an emphasis on environmental issues. Frank is considering working in private practice in New York City for 2L summer if, during his 1L summer, he works at a public interest organization. His long-term goal after graduation is to practice in an area of law in which he feels he is doing something valuable for society.

Alyssa Gonzales: Miami, Florida, is home to Alyssa as well as her geographic target area. She graduated from a small liberal arts college in the Northeast with a degree in Anthropology and an interdisciplinary minor in Ethnic Studies. Since much of her work experience prior to law school was in the public interest area, Alyssa would like to practice law with a private firm specializing in family law, with an emphasis on international adoptions. For 1L summer, Alyssa would like to work as an intern for a federal judge or with a small private practice firm in Miami. For 2L summer, Alyssa is considering working with a state or regional firm vs. a national or international firm. Her future goals include working with one or two colleagues to form a law firm with a focus on family law, including adoption law.

Denise Hollander: Denise graduated from a large state school in Florida with a degree in Mass Communications and a focus on magazine journalism. She would like to practice law with a private firm and has an interest in intellectual property, specifically trademark and copyright law, as well as media law. Her goal for 1L summer is to secure a position with a private law firm in her target area of St. Louis. Denise's goals for 2L summer depend on the outcome of her 1L summer. Overall, Denise would like to practice in a large private law firm.

Laura Mackey: Laura is from southern California and graduated from a University of California state school with a degree in Political Science and Law and Society. She attended community college before transferring to the University of California. Laura's target geographic area is St. Louis or the East Coast, especially Boston. For her 1L summer, Laura would like to work in a public legal organization that focuses on criminal law, such as a District Attorney or U.S. Attorney office. Assuming that she works in a public legal organization for 1L summer, Laura would like to work with a private law firm for her 2L summer. Future goals include working as a state or federal prosecutor.

2–3 Years Work Experience Between Undergraduate and Law School:

Abena Alemayheu: Abena's hometown is near Atlanta, Georgia. She graduated from her state university with a major in International Affairs, and worked for AmeriCorps for one year prior to law school. Her target geographic area is a major metropolitan city, preferably in the Northeast, such as D.C. or New York City. Abena plans to pursue a career in international aid and development. For her 1L summer, she would like to attend a study abroad program in a developing country where she could work in a public interest organization. For her 2L summer, Abena is thinking about trying to secure an internship with the United Nations or U.S.A.I.D., or working for the State Department.

Her long-term goals include working for an NGO that focuses on sustainable financial practices for developing countries.

Sally Nathan: Sally is from St. Louis and hopes to practice law in a major metropolitan area, including Los Angeles, Denver, or D.C. She graduated with degrees in Political Science and Journalism. Prior to attending law school, she worked for two years in a large software company in Dallas. Sally would like to spend her 1L summer in Los Angeles working in private practice, specifically in the sports and entertainment area, or in oil and gas law, with an emphasis on litigation. Sally's goals for 2L summer depend on her 1L summer experience. Her future goals include working in a large private practice firm.

Timothy Newstead: Tim was a pre-med major at a major Midwestern private university, and has an undergraduate degree in Science Pre-professional Studies. Prior to law school, Tim worked for three years as a teacher and a law clerk. His target geographic areas are Chicago and San Francisco. For his 1L summer, Tim would like to work in a public defender's office doing criminal law. While he is not ruling out private practice — perhaps in the patent law area, given his science background — Tim's focus is on practicing criminal law. His goal for his 2L summer is to work in a public defender's office. Tim's future goals include practicing in a legal organization in which he feels good about the work he is doing. He anticipates that he would work in a public defender's office for several years and then transition to private practice.

Matthew Novack: Matt is from the New York City area, and hopes to return for his legal career. He graduated with a degree in Psychology from a major research university in Boston, and worked for two years as a counselor, market research analyst, and researcher with a forensic psychologist before attending law school. Matt is interested in pursuing a career in private practice, with an emphasis on corporate law, both in the litigation and transactional areas. His goal for 1L summer is to secure a summer associate position with a large New York City law firm, and to spend 2L summer as a summer associate with either the same or a different firm. His future goal is to be a partner in a large private law firm.

Carrie Yu: Carrie received a B.A. from a major research university in Washington, D.C., with concentrations in Government and Psychology. Prior to law school, Carrie worked for two years as a paralegal in the litigation group of a large New York City law firm. Carrie's goal for 1L summer is to secure a summer associate position in Washington, D.C. with a large private law firm, in the litigation area. For her 2L summer, she would prefer to work in New York City. After graduation, Carrie plans to work in a large law firm and eventually start her own litigation firm with one or two colleagues.

More Than 3 Years Work Experience Between Undergraduate and Law School:

Alan Jacobs: Alan is from Texas. He worked for seven years before law school, as a university debate coach, a personal banker in a major U.S. bank, and a manager at a major car rental company. Alan has an undergraduate degree in Business Administration — Law from a private university in Los Angeles. His geographic target areas are Los Angeles, Chicago, New York City, or Washington, D.C. He would like to work in a large private law firm doing corporate work, preferably in the litigation area, although he is also considering transactional work. His goal for 1L summer is to secure a summer associate position in a law firm in one of his target cities. For his 2L summer, Alan anticipates choosing a firm more specific to his practice area interests, which he expects to identify over the next year. Alan's future goal is to be a partner at a large law firm.

Joanna Quinlan: Joanna is a former member of the military and worked in the Navy for ten years prior to law school. Additionally, she started her own business in the specialty bath product area. Joanna is from California, but her target geographic area is St. Louis. She graduated with a degree in Political Science from the University of California. At this time Joanna is interested in exploring opportunities as a prosecutor in the U.S. Attorney's office, as well as private practice. She is interested in criminal law, contract law, and employment law. Her goal for 1L summer is to work as a summer associate in a private law firm. Her goal for 2L summer depends on her experiences during her 1L summer. Joanna's future goal is to work as a U.S. Attorney.

Stacy Stevens: Stacy's hometown is in the South. She graduated from a major research university in Houston with a degree in Sociology. Before attending law school, she taught second grade through Teach for America and worked for a worldwide organization that involved traveling to eleven countries in one year. Stacy's target geographic areas are Washington, D.C., Chicago, and Atlanta. She is primarily interested in public interest law (with a focus on civil rights, international human rights, and anti-human trafficking law), working with refugees, and litigating wrongful conviction cases. Stacy's goal for 1L summer is to work in the public interest area, specifically for an international justice non-profit organization or for legal aid. Her goal for 2L summer will depend on her 1L summer experiences as well as the clinical courses she plans to take her 2L year. Her future goal includes having a job that allows her to balance work with her other interests, preferably in a non-profit legal organization that combines social work and administrative work. She does not plan to practice litigation directly.

Appendix C

Final Resumes

Final

Sample resume of Frank Douglas (0–1 year experience).

School Address:
1234 Lindell Blvd., Apt. W-504
St. Louis, MO 63108

Frank D. Douglas
(609) 123-4567
fddouglas@wustl.edu

Permanent Address:
18 Chase Ct.
Lawrenceville, NJ 08648

EDUCATION

Washington University School of Law   St. Louis, MO – 2018
J.D. Candidate
- Recipient - Scholar in Law Award ($X/year merit scholarship)
- Board Member - Energy and Environmental Law Society
- Member - International Law Society

Columbia University   New York, NY – 2014
B.A., Economics and Philosophy
- Dean's List - Fall 2013 & Spring 2014
- Op-Ed Writer - Columbia Spectator (school newspaper)
- Member - Columbia Democrats

PROFESSIONAL EXPERIENCE

Lutheran Social Ministries of New Jersey   Trenton, NJ – 2015
ESL Teacher
Taught adult classes in English. Worked with groups of varying ability to improve their grammar and vocabulary. Assisted in developing lessons and evaluating student ability through written and verbal tests. Taught citizenship classes to students attempting to gain U.S. citizenship, with lessons in history and civics.

Institute for Advanced Study   Princeton, NJ – 2013-2014
Public Affairs Intern
Reviewed and edited press releases. Updated website page on faculty publications and ran Excel functions to find anomalies in database cataloging term lengths of over 300 scholars. Collected biographical and autobiographical material on multiple faculty members. Drafted summaries of faculty members' life and work in preparation for retirement celebrations. Reviewed lists of scholars arriving from other institutions to make sure international institution names had been translated correctly.

Columbia University   New York, NY – 2011-2012
Information Technology General Assistant
Assisted IT department in hardware repairs and software installations on staff computers. Contacted Dell and Hewlett-Packard for information on warranties and to order replacements for malfunctioning material still covered under warranty.

American School in Japan   Tokyo, Japan – 2009
Camp Counselor
Responsible for group of 15 children aged 10-13. Assisted them in activities designed to aid them in learning English. Met with parents to discuss progress of children.

SPECIAL INTERESTS
American literature (Hemingway especially) and film (Film Noir, French New Wave)
Fan of football and soccer (played both in high school)
Member of Alumni Association of the Lawrenceville School, in NJ

LANGUAGES
Fluent in Italian and French
Reading knowledge of Spanish

Final

Sample resume of Alyssa Gonzales (0–1 year experience).

Alyssa A. Gonzales
83 Crescent
Miami, FL 33154
(305) 123-4567
alyssagonzales@wustl.edu

EDUCATION

Washington University School of Law, St. Louis, MO, *JD Candidate*   Spring 2018
Cumulative GPA: X.XX
Honors and Activities:
- Recipient – Scholars in Law Merit Award ($X/year)
- Pro Bono Committee Member – Public Service Advisory Board (branch of Student Bar Association)
- Member of Auction Committee – Women's Law Caucus
- Participant – 1L Client Counseling Competition

Davidson College, Davidson, NC, *B.A. in Anthropology, Interdisciplinary Minor in Ethnic Studies*   Spring 2014
Honors and Activities:
- Spanish Assistant Teacher and Tutor
- Staff Writer – *The Davidsonian* (school newspaper)
- Career Development Ambassador – Center for Career Development
- Treasurer – Connor House (handled > $100,000 raised for Friends for an Earlier Breast Cancer Test)
- Lector and Active Member – Catholic Campus Ministry
- Davidson in Shanghai Program at Fudan University – performed ethnographic research in Taipei, Beijing, Nanjing, Suzhou, Xi'an, Meixian, and Shanghai (Fall 2012)

EXPERIENCE

American Civil Liberties Union, Racial Justice Program, National Office, New York, NY   Fall 2014–Summer 2015
Legal Assistant
- Conducted research on potential and active cases throughout filing process
- Produced and maintained data analysis charts and legal memoranda on police reports and court dockets
- Blue Booked and cite checked legal memoranda
- Case docket and research projects included: debtor's prisons in Georgia (*Thompson v. Dekalb County*) and Mississippi; Indian Child Welfare Act in South Dakota (*Oglala Sioux Tribe v. Van Hunnik*); racial profiling in Florida, Missouri, and Wisconsin, and disparate impact and discrimination as result of intake of Big Data

Eleventh Judicial Circuit of Florida, Miami, FL   Summer 2013
Judicial Intern, Judge Mari Sampedro-Iglesia, Juvenile Dependency Judge, Human Trafficking, Unified Family Court
- Drafted motions and orders

Miami-Dade County State Attorney's Office, Miami, FL   Summer 2012
Victim-Witness Unit Intern
- Contacted victims, witnesses, lead officers, and attorneys to arrange court dates and subpoenas
- Gathered and distilled information from Next of Kin (NOK) meetings with family members of victims
- Translated from English to Spanish during court hearings and trials for some NOK

Department of Homeland Security at the Port of Miami, Miami, FL   Summer 2011
Undergraduate Intern
- Reviewed, analyzed, and organized legal documentation and files in preparation for court hearings
- Note: First undergraduate intern for DHS in Miami; assisted in developing program for future interns

Congresswoman Ileana Ros-Lehtinen, Miami, FL   Summer 2011
Congressional Intern
- Answered constituents' questions on legal documents and Congresswoman's platforms
- Trained new interns upon completion of internship

COMMUNITY INVOLVEMENT

Cuban Bar Association - Florida
Association of Women Lawyers
Carrollton Alumni Lawyer's Association

LANGUAGE

Fluent in Spanish

Final

Sample resume of Denise Hollander (0–1 year experience).

DENISE ALYSSA HOLLANDER
1234 West Pine Blvd #10L ● St. Louis, MO 63108
dahollander@wustl.edu
(941) 123-4567

EDUCATION

Washington University School of Law	**St. Louis**
J.D. Candidate	**May 2018**

Honors & Activities
Recipient: Dean's Fellowship Award (top 1L honor providing faculty and alumna mentor and research assistantship)
Recipient: The Cyrus P. & Jennie Austin Endowed Memorial Scholar in Law Award ($X tuition scholarship)
Appointed 1L Representative: Jewish Law Society
1L Representative: LearnLeo (online platform providing case-briefing and outlining tools for students)
Member: Phi Alpha Delta Legal Fraternity

University of South Florida	**Tampa**
B.A. in Mass Communications, *summa cum laude*	**Dec. 2014**

Concentration: Magazine Journalism
Selected Honors
Recipient: King O'Neal Scholar Award (awarded based on X.X GPA)
Recipient: Top Scholar Award, Kappa Tau Alpha (National Journalism Honor Society)
Recipient: John & Jerry Wing Alexander Endowed Scholarship, USF Mass Communications
Recipient: Bullitzer Prize, USF First Year Composition Program

LEGALLY RELATED EXPERIENCE

Law Office of Theodore A. Gollnick, P.A., *Legal Intern*	**Sarasota**
	2010-2015
	Part time

- Drafted Proof of Service of Annual Guardianship Reports and proposed Orders
- E-filed Annual Guardianship Reports
- Obtained certified orders from Clerk's Office
- Conducted online court record and docket searches
- Drafted Petitions for Orders Authorizing Fees and Expenses

RESEARCH & WRITING EXPERIENCE

The Israel Project, *Media Fellow*	**Washington, D.C.**
	Summer 2013

- Drafted weekly 2,000-word articles and revised same based on mentor's feedback
- Researched current events in Israel & Middle East and drafted daily blog posts
- Worked with key staff members through rotations in Press, Social Media, and Research divisions
- Participated in weekly idea flow seminars with journalists, experts, and policymakers
- Publication: *Israel's Acts of Charity Prove it is a Righteous Nation*, Algemeiner, Sept. 25, 2013

Committee for Accuracy in Middle East Reporting in America, *Campus Fellow*	**Tampa**
	2013-2014

- Drafted op-eds and letters-to-the-editor for campus and local news outlets
- Organized educational events on University of South Florida campus
- Participant: CAMERA Annual Leadership and Advocacy Training Mission to Israel

USF Holocaust & Genocide Studies/Special & Digital Collections, *Research Assistant*	**Tampa**
	2012-2013

SELECTED LEADERSHIP EXPERIENCE

Elected Vice President: USF Hillel (Recipient: Outstanding Volunteer Award)	**2013-2014**
Recipient: Activist of the Year Award, AIPAC Policy Conference	**2013**
Campus Liaison & Session Leader: Future Leaders for Israel Conference	**2014**

COMMUNITY ENGAGEMENT

Jewish National Fund Alternative Spring Break in Israel	**2014**
Kennel Enrichment Volunteer: Humane Society of Missouri	**2015**

Final

Sample resume of Laura Mackey (0–1 year experience).

Laura Mary Mackey

123 Westgate Ave #6   805.123.4567
St. Louis, MO 63130   lmm@wustl.edu

Education

Washington University School of Law   **St. Louis, MO**
J.D. Candidate   May 2018
   Honors and Activities
     Recipient: Scholar of Law Scholarship (merit-based, $X/year for 3 years)
     Member: Women's Law Caucus; American Constitution Society
     Participant: Client Counseling Competition

University of California, Riverside   **Riverside, CA**
B.A., Political Science, Law and Society, *summa cum laude*   June 2015
   Honors and Activities
     Recipient: Dean's Honor List (3 consecutive quarters with GPA of at least X.X) and Dean's Academic
       Distinction Award (required GPA of at least X.X)
     Vice President (elected position, 2014-2015); member (2013-2015) - Mock Trial
       As Vice President team won Honorable Mention at local competition (1st time for UCR). Worked with team
       members to improve direct and cross-examination questions and techniques. Organized and ran practices.

Santa Barbara City College   **Santa Barbara, CA**
A.A., Political Science   May 2013
     Recipient: President's Honor List (required GPA of at least X.X)

Boston University   **Boston, MA**
                                                                     May 2008

Legally Related Experience

United States Pretrial Services   **Riverside, CA**
Intern   January 2014-June 2014
     Observed U.S. Pretrial Officers during initial bail hearings, bail reviews, and inmate interviews. Verified
     criminal records. Coordinated inmate intake with federal agencies including FBI, DEA, U.S. Marshals.

Santa Barbara Superior Court   **Santa Barbara, CA**
Own Recognizance Investigator   October 2011-August 2013
     Began as an intern and promoted to paid Judicial Assistant II within four months. Interviewed inmates at county
     jail and drafted custody status reports for judges. Reviewed inmates' prior criminal records. Reviewed Probable
     Cause Declarations and submitted to judges. Completed bail increase/reduction documents and release
     paperwork and submitted documents to custody officers. Researched Los Angeles County bail schedule. Served
     as liaison between Court and sheriff's department, police department, probation officers, and parole officers.
     Assisted inmates and their friends/family in understanding and navigating the legal process.

Other Professional Experience

Jackson Medical Group   **Santa Barbara, CA**
(General Practice Group with 12 physicians in 4 offices)
Billing Assistant   October 2008-June 2012
     Submitted records of patients' visits to insurance companies. Deposited and balanced insurance payments.
     Worked with major national insurance companies such as Blue Cross, Blue Shield, Cigna, and AARP as well as
     Medicare. All tasks complied with HIPAA regulations. Assisted patients in resolving conflicts with insurance
     companies.

Interests
     Ran two marathons. Hiked Mt. Whitney (14,509 ft., highest mountain in contiguous United States).

Foreign Language
     Spanish
       Speaking: Limited Working Proficiency. Reading: Limited Working Proficiency.

Final

Sample resume of Abena Alemayheu (2–3 years experience).

ABENA O. ALEMAYHEU

7274 Dartmouth Avenue Apt 2E
University City, MO 63130

a.alemayheu@wustl.edu
404.550.5497

EDUCATION

WASHINGTON UNIVERSITY SCHOOL OF LAW, St. Louis, Missouri
J.D   May 2018

HONORS AND ACTIVITIES
- Recipient: Virginia Morsey Talley Scholarship (Merit-based scholarship covering $X tuition for 3 years)
- 1L Elected Representative: Student Bar Association
- Member: Education Committee for the Public Service Advisory Board
- Member: Women's Law Caucus, Black Law Student Association, International Law Society
- Participant: Client Counseling Competition

UNIVERSITY OF GEORGIA, Athens, GA   May 2013
- Bachelor of Arts, International Affairs, *cum laude*
- Minor: Sociology

HONORS AND ACTIVITIES
- Recipient: Hope Scholarship (Merit-based scholarship covering $X tuition)
- Recipient: Pell Grant (Need-based grant for living expenses)
- Member: World Ambassador, National Residence, Hall Honorary, Residence Hall Association, Mentor

TEACHING AND MENTORING EXPERIENCE

YOUTH VILLAGES AMERICORPS, Douglasville, GA   September 2014-July 2015
National Service Member
- Completed 1,700 hours of service at a residential treatment facility for youth with severe emotional/behavioral issues
- Provided one-on-one weekly tutoring sessions to students focusing on core subjects at an accredited Title I school and designed innovative out-of-school hour enrichment activities focusing on culture, health, science, and problem solving
- Created a service learning project that incorporated common core standards and community service in collaboration with at-risk students, facilitated Student Council to provide youth leadership opportunities, and leveraged external volunteers to meet campus and community needs
- Ensured member compliance with housing rules and safety regulations as lead campsite liaison

WORLD LEADER, Athens, GA   Summer 2012
International Student Orientation Leader (Competitive Selection)
- Hosted presentation for incoming international students through Office of International Student Life, contributed to presentations about campus life, and served as a mentor

CIVIC ENGAGEMENT EXPERIENCE

IMPACT CENTER FOR LEADERSHIP & SERVICE
Bluefield, WV, Service Trip Participant – Theme: Ageism   March 2013
- Provided tutoring in Math and English for students ages 10-14 and engaged older adults in conversation and recreational activities at local senior center

Asheboro, NC, Service Trip Participant – Theme: Affordable Housing   March 2012
- Assisted in constructing house with Habitat for Humanity and provided support to organization's team located on the premises

SKILLS

Certifications: CPR, First Aid, FEMA Disaster Response, Project WET (Water Education), WILD (Environmental Conservation), and Learning Tree (Environmental Education), Ropes Course Facilitator
Languages: Arabic (elementary proficiency) and Spanish (elementary proficiency)

Final

Sample resume of Sally Nathan (2–3 years experience).

Sally Nathan

123 Lake Drive   (314) 123-4567
Kirkwood, MO 63122   snathan@wustl.edu

EDUCATION

Washington University School of Law   St. Louis, MO
J.D. Candidate: May 2018
Honors and Activities:
> Winner – 1L Client Competition (70 teams)
> 1L Elected Representative – Student Bar Association
> 1L Elected Representative – Phi Alpha Delta
> Member – Wash U Out West (WOW)
> Member – Sports and Entertainment Law Society

University of Kansas   Lawrence, KS
B.S., Journalism, May 2013 – GPA: X.XX
Honors and Activities:
> Recruit - Heptathlete – D1 Track and Field
> Medalist - All Big 12 Track and Field
> Recipient - Jayhawk Generations Scholarship
> Member - National Society for Collegiate Scholars
> Member and Technology Chair – Pi Beta Phi

Sant Jordi University   Barcelona, Spain
Language, Literature and Culture Study Abroad Program   Summer 2013

LEGALLY RELATED AND BUSINESS EXPERIENCE

ISNetworld Software Corporation   Dallas, TX
Senior Associate   July 2014–June 2015
Reviewed OSHA documents (300A and 300log), workers' compensation claims, insurance documents (including general and employers' liability) and safety programs for regulatory compliance. Primary account manager for large clients in Oil and Gas Industry (Kinder Morgan, Plains All American, TransCanada, Alliance Pipelines, Plains Midstream Canada). Developed and presented programs to potential contractors (200-300 attendees) regarding clients' compliance requirements. Team lead during management meetings and prospective client meetings for senior management of Oil and Gas companies. Position involved extensive travel throughout the United States and Canada.
Associate   August 2013–July 2014
Communicated and deescalated customer conflicts in person and via phone. Researched and drafted customer case studies for company website. Trained new employees on company protocols.

Fuksa Khorshid, LLC   Chicago, IL
Legal Intern   June 2012–August 20
Assisted partner during depositions and client meetings. Appointed as co-chair for fundraiser event that raised more than $50,000 for Chicago Charities. Attended hearings in small claims court.

OTHER LEADERSHIP AND COMMUNITY ENGAGEMENT

OSHA Oil and Gas Conference   Houston, TX
Volunteer: December 2014
Responsible for registration of 2,000+ attendees. Interfaced/worked with OSHA and Oil and Gas representatives.

Natural Ties Volunteer Program   Lawrence, KS
Volunteer: August 2009–May 2013
Interacted with mentally challenged seniors through variety of weekly activities.

INTERESTS

Violinist, Equestrian (hunter/jumper), Runner (half marathons), Softball

Final

Sample resume of Timothy Newstead (2–3 years experience).

Timothy J. Newstead

7424 Buckingham Dr., Apt. 2D, St. Louis, MO 63105 ~ (314) 123-4567 ~ newsteadt@wustl.edu

EDUCATION

Washington University in St. Louis School of Law   St. Louis, MO
Juris Doctor Candidate   May 2018
Honors: Recipient - Scholar in Law Merit-Based Scholarship ($X/year for 3 years)
Activities: Participant - 1L Client Counseling and Interviewing Competition
                   Member - Public Service Advisory Board and Public Service Committee

University of Notre Dame   Notre Dame, IN
Bachelor of Science in Science Pre-Professional: GPA X.XX   May 2012
Honors: University of Notre Dame Dean's List (Fall 2009)
Activities: Member - Friends of the Orphans Club (public service organization); Participant -
                   Interhall Football (full pad, tackle football – safety and kicker); Member - Bengal Bouts
                   Boxing Club; Member - Pre-Professional Society

Southern Methodist University   Dallas, TX
GPA: X.X/4.0   Fall 2008-Spring 2009

LEGALLY RELATED EXPERIENCE

Elman Law Group, LLC (Boutique Personal Injury Law Firm)   Chicago, IL
Law Clerk   2014-2015
Researched Illinois lien law and state laws relating to estate law and real property. Negotiated liens on
behalf of clients with lien holders, including health care providers and insurance companies. Drafted motions
to adjudicate liens and filed motions with Circuit Court. Drafted correspondence and communicated via
telephone with clients regarding status of cases, including updates on settlement negotiations,
court dates and depositions. Drafted letters to referring attorneys noting status of cases.

TEACHING AND RESEARCH EXPERIENCE

Passionist Volunteers International – Jamaica   Mandeville, Jamaica
Orientation Leader, Teacher, Soccer Coach   2012-2013; 2014
Taught group of 5-year-old students with learning challenges in reading, writing, and math. Mentored
boys at St. John Bosco Boy's Home, group home for at-risk youth, and coached Under 18 soccer team.
Led retreats for Jamaican youth at St. Paul Catholic Retreat House. Invited by program director to assist
in four-week-long orientation program. Initiated new volunteers into way of life for PVIs in Jamaica.
Mentored outgoing volunteers on coping with leaving after service year.

Washington University Medical School (Anesthesiology Department at St. Louis Children's Hospital)   St. Louis, MO
Intern   2011
Designed database using Microsoft Access to organize quality improvement data. Data provided doctors
with feedback from patients regarding patient care. Shadowed anesthesiologists at St. Louis Children's
Hospital. Helped with orientation for M3 students and interns. Assisted orientation director with
set-up for mock patient room which presented students with scenarios on how to deal with patient emergencies.

COMMUNITY ENGAGEMENT

Memorial Hospital   South Bend, IN
Ambassador   2012
Volunteered in pediatric unit of hospital. Worked with Child Life Specialist and provided support for
patients and families.

Slice of Life Club at University of Notre Dame   South Bend, IN
Tutor   2011-2012
Tutored children ages 5-13 in math and reading. Developed positive relationships with
children and served as mentor.

SKILLS & INTERESTS

Language: Working proficiency in French
Interests: Notre Dame football, golf, reading (John Le Carré, Dennis Lehane, Alan Furst, Ken Follett),
                   and writing (blog about College Football and wrote two screenplays at Notre Dame)

Final

Sample resume of Matthew Novack (2–3 years experience).

Matthew T. Novack
(845) 123-4567 mtnovack@wustl.edu

Permanent Address: School Address:
16 Adams Court, Nanuet, NY 10954   7025 Forsyth Dr., St. Louis, MO 63105

EDUCATION
Washington University School of Law, JD Candidate   *May 2018*
Honors and Activities
- Recipient: Scholar in Law (merit-based XX% tuition scholarship for three years)
- Recipient: William R. and Nancy J. Hirsch Scholarship (merit-based XX% tuition scholarship for three years)
- 1L Elected Representative: IP Law Society
- 1L Appointed Representative: Employment Law Society
- Participant: Client Counseling & Interviewing Competition
- Member: Negotiation and Dispute Resolution Society

Boston University, B.A., Psychology   *May 2013*
Honors and Activities
- Dean's List
- Member: Kappa Sigma Fraternity
- Member: Sigma Alpha Lambda Honor Society

LAW-RELATED EXPERIENCE
Office of Frederick Winsmann, PhD, Clinical and Forensic Psychologist, Boston, Massachusetts.
Forensic Psychology Research Assistant   *March 2014 – Present*
Research and analyze criminal and behavioral patterns using legal, medical, and personal records for use in forensic reports to help evaluate criminal responsibility, risk of reoffending, competency to stand trial, and SVP civil commitment. Draft sections of forensic reports for submission to federal and state courts. Review and incorporate legal documents and research statutes pertaining to mental health commitment and competency to stand trial. Adhere to strict industry standards of quality and confidentiality. File trademark application with USPTO for continuing education symposium on psychology and the law.

Rockland County District Court, New City, New York.
Judicial Intern   *Summer 2012*
Observed criminal trials and hearings, and meetings between assistant district attorneys, defense attorneys, and judges. Performed basic legal research and discussed relevant matters of case law pertaining to current cases with judge. Relayed information between judges, clerks, and attorneys.

BUSINESS EXPERIENCE
Avention, Inc. (Formerly OneSource Information Services – 200+ employees), Concord, Massachusetts.
Market Research Analyst   *March 2014–August 2015*
Researched and analyzed competitive intelligence information including corporate strategy and risk, research and development expenditures, emerging markets, strategic initiatives, corporate restructuring, enterprise information technology infrastructure composition and requirements, intra-company production and development methodologies (Six-Sigma, Agile, Waterfall, Scrum). Analyzed SEC filings, annual reports, quarterly reports, corporate finances and earnings calls. Researched financial and information technology trends on enterprise- and industry-wide scale. Tracked corporate capital expenditures with an emphasis on IT software and hardware expenditures. Maintained, purged, and regularly updated database information. Used enterprise content management system to publish quarterly custom market research reports on more than 100 Fortune 1000 companies in dozens of industries.

OTHER PROFESSIONAL EXPERIENCE
Advocates, Inc., Dedham, Massachusetts.

Direct Care Counselor   *May 2013–December 2013*
Assisted in the design and implementation of individualized mental health treatment plans. Helped evaluate patients for psychological symptoms and effectiveness of prescribed medication.

INTERESTS: Boating, swimming, wakeboarding, waterskiing, snowboarding, and playing guitar.

Final

Sample resume of Carrie Yu (2–3 years experience).

Carrie S. Yu

12 South Kingshighway Blvd., Apt. 12S, St. Louis, MO 63108 | (703) 123-4567 | carriesyu@wustl.edu

EDUCATION

WASHINGTON UNIVERSITY SCHOOL OF LAW — St. Louis, MO
J.D. Candidate — May 2018
Honors: Scholar in Law Award (merit-based $X tuition scholarship for all three years)
Activities: 1L Representative – Asian Pacific American Law Students Association
Member – Women's Law Caucus
Participant – 1L Client Counseling Competition

GEORGETOWN UNIVERSITY — Washington, DC
B.A., majors in Government and Psychology, *cum laude* — May 2013
Honors: Psychology Departmental Honors
Thesis: *The Effect of the Addition of a Semantically Meaningful Context & Language on the Video Deficit Effect*
Activities: Secretary – Class of 2013 Committee
Member – Habitat for Humanity (3 years)
Member – College Peer Advisors (2 years)

UNIVERSITY COLLEGE LONDON — London, England
Semester Abroad (including significant research and writing courses culminating in thesis) — Spring 2012
Thesis: *Culture, Power, and Inhibition: An Examination of the Effect of Power on Inhibition in Asian Populations*

PUBLICATIONS & PRESENTATIONS

- Zimmermann L, Moser A, Grenell A, Dickerson K, Yao Q, Gerhardstein P and Barr R (2015) Do semantic contextual cues facilitate transfer learning from video in toddlers? *Front. Psychol.* 6:561. doi:10.3389/fpsyg.2015.00561
- Dickerson K, Oot E, Yao Q, Barr R, Gerhardstein P (2012) *The effect of instructions on imitation from live and video demonstrations.* Poster presentation at the International Conference on Infant Studies, Minneapolis MN

LEGAL EXPERIENCE

PAUL, WEISS, RIFKIND, WHARTON & GARRISON LLP — New York, NY
Litigation Paralegal — June 2013–July 2015
- Supervised and managed team of 30 paralegals, as lead paralegal, of foreclosure case.
- Conducted research and prepared documents for filings, depositions, hearings, and trial, for nine-month, multi-billion dollar environmental damages trial.

SIGNIFICANT RESEARCH AND WRITING EXPERIENCE

GEORGETOWN UNIVERSITY EARLY LEARNING PROJECT — Washington, DC
Undergraduate Psychology Research Assistant — Jan 2011–May 2013
- Collected and analyzed data on early childhood learning from television and touchscreens.

GEORGETOWN UNIVERSITY GOVERNMENT DEPARTMENT — Washington, DC
Undergraduate Government Research Assistant — Sept 2012–Dec 2012
- Drafted memos on multi-state policies regarding abstinence-only sex education.

GEORGETOWN UNIVERSITY WRITING CENTER — Washington, DC
Writing Tutor and English Teaching Assistant (Competitive Selection) — Sept 2010–May 2011
- Read and revised undergraduate and graduate students' papers. Recommended improvements to students' writing.

COMMUNITY ENGAGEMENT

WILDWOOD SUMMER THEATER — Bethesda, MD
Director of Fundraising — June 2012–Aug 2012
- Headed the fundraising efforts of 501c(3) theater company and exceeded fundraising goal of $20,000.

SPIRIT FOUNDATION (Scholarship Foundation Founded in Memory of High School Classmate) — Rockville, MD
Board Member — May 2010–May 2011
- Fundraised for annual $5000 college scholarship for graduating high school senior.

SPECIAL SKILLS & INTERESTS

Chinese (Fluent) ◆ Level 6 Pianist ◆ Photography (Winner of Online Contests) ◆ Firm Volleyball Team ◆ Musical Theater Enthusiast

Final

Sample resume of Alan Jacobs (more than 3 years experience).

ALAN C. JACOBS
6822 Oakland Ave. Apt: 104 St. Louis, MO 63139
Cell: 210-123-4567 | acjacobs@wustl.edu

EDUCATION

Washington University School of Law   St. Louis, MO
J.D. Candidate   *Current*
- GPA: X.XX (Top 1/3 = X.XX)
- Recipient - Merit-based scholarship (XX% tuition/year)
- Finalist - Client Counseling Competition (top XX%)
- Elected Academic Chair - Phi Alpha Delta
- Member - Federalist Society, Intellectual Property Law Society, Energy and Environmental Law Society

Loyola Marymount University   Los Angeles, CA
B.A. Business Law emphasis   *2009*
- Recipient - Merit-based scholarship (XX% tuition/year)
- Founder - Royal Debate Society – Non-profit organization teaching communication to middle school Korean ESL students; Developed curriculum and negotiated need based scholarships among universities
- Elected President - Loyola Debate Team (managed 100 members)

PROFESSIONAL EXPERIENCE

Winston Churchill High School   San Antonio, TX
Assistant Debate Coach   *2012-2015*
- Facilitated personalized communication training with emphasis on judge adaptation, oral argumentation strategy, and general communication skills; Selected to present material at University of North Texas Summer Debate Camp to students and coaches from across United States
- Selected by coaches and students to judge Texas State Finals (largest state tournament nationally)
- Accomplished team goal: every varsity member qualified for State, every varsity member achieved 1st place, sent students to Nationals every year – previously 1/6 varsity members attended State

U.S. Bank   Los Angeles, CA
Personal Banker   *2011-2012*
- Surpassed top 10% in sales for 4Q11; Acquired 40 new clients and advised clients on $1.3M in assets
- Modified and implemented performance tracker and loan calculator resulting in 87% office growth in 2012
- Appointed district representative for internal regional newsletter; Restructured newspaper content, coordinated cross divisional information, drafted district specific articles
- Appointed corporate account representative

Enterprise Rent-A-Car   Los Angeles, CA / San Antonio, TX
Assistant Manager   *2009-2011*
- Designed and executed marketing strategy resulting in 49% office growth (2nd highest in South Texas)
- Improved relations with four key accounts worth $1.7M resulting in $200K revenue growth
- Managed employees at 3rd largest office in Los Angeles grossing $3.2M/year in revenue
- Mentored 14 employees to pass their management qualification test, including two hour interview addressing legal liabilities of managing business and terms of rental contract

Management Trainee   *2007-2009*
- L.A. MVP 15 times for sales; Led team to set performance records at 3 different locations
- Negotiated and drafted proposals to open office projected at $1.2M revenue/year and to acquire business from ten new accounts; Projects required working closely with senior management
- Appointed district corporate account representative; Maintained and facilitated growth for 25% of region's corporate accounts

SKILLS AND INTERESTS

- Proficient in creating complex databases in Excel
- Art, Philosophy, Reading Classical Literature and Science Fiction
- Club and Intramural Soccer, Hiking, Fishing

Final

Sample resume of Joanna Quinlan (more than 3 years experience).

Joanna Natasha Quinlan

6719 Melrose Avenue, Unit A   (312) 123-4567
St. Louis, MO 63119   j.n.quinlan@wustl.edu

Education
Washington University School of Law   **St. Louis, Missouri**
J.D. Candidate: May 2018
Selected Honors and Activities
   Recipient – Scholar in Law (Merit-Based Scholarship covering $X/year)
   Treasurer (Elected position) - Student Veterans' Association
   Member - Women's Law Caucus; Annual Auction Donations Committee; Participant: Room at the Inn Service Project
   Member - Young Friends of Legal Services of Eastern Missouri; Participant: Lydia's House Service Project
   Member - Woman Lawyers' Association; Participant: Annual Charity Auction
University of California, Los Angeles   **Los Angeles, California**
   Bachelor of Arts, 2006
Selected Honors and Activities
     College Honors, *cum laude*
     Participant - Study Abroad Program – August 2005 through June 2006, Bilkent University, Ankara, Turkey
     Member - Bruin Democrats, Bruin Democrat Debate Team
Solano Community College   **Fairfield, California**
Selected Awards and Activities
     Participant – Debate Team
     Gold Medal Recipient: National Competition - Impromptu Speaking
     Gold Medal Recipient at California State Competition – Parliamentary Debate and Impromptu Speaking

Selected Legally Related Experience
U.S. Navy Legal Officer 2007-2014   **Various Navy Duty Stations**
Conducted investigations of violations of Uniform Code of Military Justice (UCMJ). Interviewed witnesses in connection with alleged violations of UCMJ including violations related to conspiracy, blackmail, and assault. Verbally reported findings of investigation to commanding officer for referral to Judge Advocate General Corps (JAG).
Sexual Assault Victim's Intervention (SAVI) Advocate 2007-2014   **Various Navy Duty Stations**
Worked to support victims of sexual violence in shipboard setting to ensure they were familiar with rights and services available to them. Facilitated contact with mental health and legal professionals on an as needed basis.

Selected Business Related Experience
U.S. Navy Officer 2005-2014   **Various Navy Duty Stations**
Supply/Logistics Officer – Active Duty & Reserve   **St. Louis, Missouri**
- Served as Stock Control & Information Technology Division Head managing over $12M in shipboard supplies, material, and stock (13,000 individual line items) for the USNS SAN JOSE (T-AFS 7) supporting U.S. Naval operations for warships in SEVENTH Fleet (Western Pacific & Indian Ocean) & FIFTH Fleet (Arabian Gulf).
- Managed 25 Navy logistics and IT specialists to include all elements of ordering, inventory, material inspection/receiving, spares management, depot level repairable (DLR) induction/shipment/receipt of spares, warehousing and transportation on-and-off ship, underway replenishment of warships, and supply management IT systems.
- Led vendor management for ship interfacing with over 30 foreign vendors in Guam, Japan & Okinawa, Philippines, Australia, Singapore, United Arab Emirates, and Bahrain.
- Accountable for interpreting U.S. Navy fleet customer requirements, e.g. RFIs, RFQs, Statements of Work (SOW), Supplier Statements of Work (SSOW), and RFPs, facilitating vendor selection and contract award, contractor payments, and monitoring and quality assurance of vendor and contractor performance in over six foreign countries and the U.S.
- Drafted reports on Supply Chain Metrics and presented results to officers on monthly basis.
- Drafted daily operations report for Maritime Sealift Fleet Support Command.

Wildwood Organics 2010-2014   **St. Louis, Missouri**
President and Founder
Founded small entrepreneurial business as sole proprietor. Business focused on high quality niche bath products. Served as supplier to three retailers in St. Louis region and over 270 individual customers worldwide. Averaged 30 percent margins and business grew by 200 percent over four years.

Final

Sample resume of Stacy Stevens (more than 3 years experience).

7345 Yale Ave. Apt 2E   stacyastevens@wustl.edu
St. Louis, MO 63130   504-123-4567

Stacy A. Stevens

EDUCATION

Washington University School of Law   St. Louis, Missouri
J.D. Candidate   May 2018
Honors and Activities

- Recipient - Dean's Fellowship ($X tuition for three years, faculty mentor, research assistantship)
- Finalist - 1L Client Counseling Competition (one of 24 teams out of 72 participating)
- Member - Women's Law Caucus - Auction Committee Member (largest student-led fundraiser designated for 2L public interest summer stipend)
- Member - Public Service Advisory Board-Public Service Committee; Black Law Students Association; International Law Society

Rice University   Houston, Texas
Bachelor of Arts in Sociology, magna cum laude (GPA: X.XX/4.00)   May 2011
Honors and Activities

- Inductee - *Phi Beta Kappa*
- Recipient - QuestBridge Scholarship ($X tuition and living expenses for four years)
- President - The Impact Movement (Rice chapter of national org.) - collaborated with Asst. Dean for Students to plan initiatives, drafted proposals for organization funding, served as liaison between campus and national organization, spearheaded on-campus outreach, and coordinated logistics for national conference
- Community Service Chair - Black Students Association (elected position) - coordinated community events
- Member - Advocating Diversity Association - Event Committee Member - secured sponsorship from local businesses, obtained funding from student government, and allocated facilities for program use

PUBLIC SERVICE & NON-PROFIT EXPERIENCE

The World Race   Asia, Europe, Africa
Participant and Logistics Coordinator (appointed position)   September 2013-August 2014
Traveled to 11 countries in 11 months as part of missionary team; raised $15,500 in funds through presentations and letters to board members and individual investors; partnered with local organizations and ministries to combat human trafficking, teach English, feed and clothe orphans, clean townships, and restore buildings; coordinated transportation, lodging, and administration for 40+ people; and served as liaison between on-site team and headquarters' logistics leader.

The Impact Movement   Orlando, FL
Assistant to Director of Communications   Summer 2010
Drafted promotional article for *The Orlando Times* to publicize organization; coordinated regular publishing opportunities for organization; redesigned marketing strategies; and developed conference materials for 1500 attendees.

LEGALLY RELATED EXPERIENCE

U. S. Equal Employment Opportunity Commission   Houston, TX
Legal Intern/Mentee   Summer 2009
Conducted research on case facts and witness history; reviewed legal memos and briefs for accuracy; attended witness deposition; shadowed director of district office; designed applicant database of over 300 contacts; and located witnesses.

TEACHING EXPERIENCE

Teach for America - Jackson Elementary School   Jackson, LA
Second Grade Teacher   July 2011-July 2013
Developed over 20 lessons and activities per week; facilitated student growth of 1.8 years in reading; managed 17 students in behavior and character development; created specialized plan for student needs; forged critical parent and student relationships in furtherance of common goal; and campaigned for county-wide tax initiative to benefit students.

St. Charles Parish Schools   Destrehan, LA
Substitute Teacher   August 2014-May 2015
Assisted special education students in schoolwork and recreation activities; completed individualized student plans and tracking charts; and coordinated with parents to implement student-specific goals.

SKILLS & INTERESTS

Languages: French (Limited Working Proficiency) and Spanish (Elementary Proficiency)
Alto - Gospel Choir

Appendix D

Final Cover Letters

Final

Sample cover letter of Denise Hollander (school connection).

DENISE ALYSSA HOLLANDER
1234 West Pine Blvd #10L • St. Louis, MO 63108
dahollander@wustl.edu
(941) 123-4567

January 14, 20XX

Ms. Marsha Dennis
Tucker Smith LLP
7000 Forsyth Blvd
Suite 1000
St. Louis, MO 63105

Dear Ms. Dennis:

I recently spoke with John Holmes, one of your intellectual property attorneys, at the Employer Showcase hosted by Washington University School of Law ("Wash U Law"). I also had the opportunity to attend the 1L reception hosted by Tucker Smith in December. The collaborative and welcoming atmosphere of your firm was evident to me from both of those experiences. As a recent transplant to St. Louis, I am eager to make a connection in the St. Louis legal community with a firm like yours that has a varied, sophisticated practice as well as a reputation for community engagement. Please accept this letter and my attached resume as my application for a summer internship with Tucker Smith.

I am interested in exploring your firm's wide variety of practice areas, especially intellectual property, and am excited by the opportunity to seek responsibility early on as an associate. I am confident that I have the research and writing skills, leadership skills, and enthusiasm to be an asset to Tucker Smith this summer and beyond. In addition to maintaining a strong overall academic record, ranking in the top XX% of my class, I have demonstrated my writing ability in law school by earning the highest grade in my Legal Practice course, X.X. This builds on my prior research and writing experience obtained through journalistic training at the University of South Florida and as a media fellow for multiple organizations. Moreover, I developed leadership skills while serving in a variety of capacities at my undergraduate university and in the South Florida community. In addition to building a successful legal practice, it is important to me to be involved in my community. Tucker Smith's demonstrated commitment to the St. Louis community appeals to me.

I understand that Tucker Smith is participating in the on-campus interview program at Wash U Law and I welcome the opportunity to meet with you or one of your colleagues. In the meantime, please contact me if there is any other information you need from me at this time.

Sincerely,

Denise Hollander

Denise Hollander

Encl.: resume

Final

Sample cover letter of Laura Mackey (school connection).

Laura M. Mackey
123 Westgate Ave #6
St. Louis, Missouri 63130 lmm@wustl.edu

January 10, 20XX

Missouri State Public Defender System
Attn: Gina Hall, Human Resources
Woodrail Centre
1000 West Nifong, Building 7, Suite 100
Columbia, Missouri 65203

Dear Ms. Hall,

A representative from the Missouri State Public Defender's Office (the "PD Office") spoke at Washington University School of Law's Public Service Career Fair this week. At that event, I talked to Mr. David Sanger, a public defender with your office. Mr. Sanger's enthusiasm for his work inspired me to seek an internship with the PD Office. As a first year law student I am hoping to combine my new legal skills with my experience working in the criminal justice system by working for your office this coming summer. I plan to live in the St. Louis area, but am willing to commute to another city if there is a greater need for an intern in a different location.

I am confident that my academic achievements, experience, and enthusiasm will contribute to the PD Office. This first year of law school, I am proud to have earned high grades in Criminal Law and Legal Practice, our legal analysis and writing course. In Legal Practice, I received praise for my research-based writing assignments and my oral presentation skills. Prior to law school, I worked for the Santa Barbara Superior Court Recognizance Unit. I interviewed individuals immediately after arrest with the goal of releasing them from custody without bail. While our primary task was to reduce jail population, my office was often able to help individuals who would not otherwise be able to post bail. During my time in this position, I gained an understanding of the criminal legal process. I also witnessed the impact this process can have on low-income individuals and their families. It was this experience that inspired the passion I will bring to the PD Office if given the opportunity to intern there this summer.

I will contact you in a couple of weeks to confirm that you received this letter and my enclosed resume. Before then, if you have questions regarding my qualifications, please contact me at (805) 123-4567 or at lmm@wustl.edu. Thank you in advance for your consideration. I look forward to speaking with you.

Sincerely,

Laura M. Mackey
Laura M. Mackey
Encl.: resume

Final

Sample cover letter of Matthew Novack (school connection).

Matthew T. Novack
(845) 123-4567
mtnovack@wustl.edu

School Address
7025 Forsyth Dr.
St. Louis, MO 63105

Permanent Address
16 Adams Court
Nanuet, NY 10954

January 24, 20XX

Benjamin Cruse, Esquire
Commodity Futures Trading
Commission 140 Broadway
New York, NY 10005

RE: 20XX Summer Internship Program

Dear Mr. Cruse,

Please accept the enclosed resume and personal statement as my application for the Commodity Futures Trading Commission's ("CFTC's") 20XX Summer Internship Program ("Internship"). I learned about the CFTC Internship at the Federal Government Career Fair held at my law school, Washington University in St. Louis–School of Law. I was intrigued by the opportunities that participants in the CFTC Internship have to participate in all phases of the CFTC's work. After law school, I plan to use my background in corporate work and psychology to pursue a career in securities litigation and white-collar criminal prosecution. If selected for the CFTC Internship, I welcome the opportunity to pursue my interests and to apply my corporate experience and expertise in securities research to contribute substantively to the CFTC's efforts.

Prior to law school, I worked as a market research analyst for a business information firm, where I researched corporate information technology trends and immersed myself in financial statements and SEC filings using the SEC's EDGAR database. I drafted reports on information technology and corporate expenditures in a variety of industries, using U.S. Census Bureau economic data and American FactFinder to extrapolate trends and identify growth areas. I believe that my technical understanding of corporate underpinnings and securities research experience will allow me to assist you and your colleagues at the CFTC this summer.

I welcome the opportunity to speak with you or one of your colleagues about my interest in, and qualifications for, the CFTC Internship program. I will contact you in a couple of weeks to confirm receipt of my application materials. In the meantime, please contact me at (845) 123-4567 or mtnovack@wustl.edu if you have any questions. Thank you in advance for your time and consideration.

Sincerely,

Matthew T. Novack
Matthew T. Novack

Encls.: Resume
         Statement of Interest

Final

Sample cover letter of Timothy Newstead (non-school connection).

Timothy J. Newstead
7424 Buckingham Dr., Apt. 2D
St. Louis, MO 63105

January 12, 20XX

Jane Allen, Esquire
California Appellate Project
101 Second Street, Suite 600
San Francisco, CA 94105

Dear Ms. Allen:

Sarah Volk, my friend and a former intern with the California Appellate Project (the "Appellate Project"), recommended that I apply for the 20XX summer internship. Sarah's enthusiasm for the work she did at the Appellate Project as an intern last summer inspired me to apply for an internship this summer. I am a first-year law student at Washington University in St. Louis School of Law. Like Sarah, I am committed to a career in public interest law, with an emphasis on criminal law. Please accept this letter and my enclosed resume as my application for a summer internship with the Appellate Project.

My primary goal in attending law school is to work in criminal defense, perhaps as a public defender. I am currently a member of the Public Service Advisory Board at Washington University. PSAB is a student-led organization that allocates public service funds among student groups, facilitates educational events about public service careers, creates opportunities for public service within the law school and in the larger St. Louis community, and administers the Pro Bono Pledge. I am an active member of the Public Service Committee and have had the opportunity to organize service projects to foster student involvement with the St. Louis community. My involvement with this organization has strengthened my determination to pursue a career in public service.

My commitment to public service predates law school. I spent my last two years at Notre Dame volunteering as an after-school tutor for local youth and weekly at a local hospital. I also spent a year after college living and working in Jamaica with the Passionist Volunteers International. My interest in criminal law stems from the challenges I observed many of my students enduring as their family members navigated the criminal justice system, often without consistent legal representation. I believe that spending this summer as an intern for the Appellate Project would be an incredible opportunity and the first step in realizing my goal of becoming a public defender.

I will be in Chicago during the weekend of February 6th for the Midwest Public Interest Law Career Conference, and welcome the opportunity to meet with you or one of your colleagues to discuss the Appellate Project and my qualifications for an internship with it. In the meantime, please feel free to contact me at (314) 123-4567 or newsteadt@wustl.edu. Thank you in advance for your consideration.

Sincerely,

Timothy J. Newstead

Encl.: Resume

Final

Sample cover letter of Carrie Yu (non-school connection).

Carrie S. Yu
12 South Kingshighway Blvd., Apt. 12S
St. Louis, MO 63108
(703) 123-4567
carriesyu@wustl.edu

December 18, 20XX

Ms. Valerie Rogers
Senior Manager, Recruiting & Retention
Davis Smith P.C.
1234 Main Street
Indianapolis, IN 46204

RE: <u>Davis Smith New York Internship</u>

Dear Ms. Rogers,

I met Sarah Jones from your firm's New York office at the National Asian Pacific American Bar Association Conference in New Orleans this November, and she encouraged me to apply for a 1L summer associate position in the firm's New York office. Ms. Jones's enthusiasm for her labor and employment practice at Davis Smith, as well as the firm's demonstrated dedication to diversity, is very appealing to me. I worked in New York for two years before attending law school and plan to return to the area after graduation. I believe I am a very strong candidate for a summer associate position with your firm for a number of reasons.

My research and writing skills, prior work experience, and ability to work in a fast-paced environment will be assets in this position. This fall, at the end of my first semester in law school, I received the highest grade in my Legal Practice (research and writing) section. This grade was based on multiple research and writing assignments. For the two years prior to law school, I worked as a Litigation Paralegal at a large, sophisticated New York City law firm. In that position, I supervised a team of paralegals in connection with a nationwide class-action lawsuit involving thousands of documents. I know that my attention to detail, perfectionist personality, and strong work ethic are characteristics that will allow me to succeed in the fast-paced environment of Davis Smith.

I will be in New York during the first week of January and welcome the opportunity to meet with you or your colleagues to discuss my qualifications for a summer associate position with Davis Smith. I will contact you in a couple of weeks to confirm that you received this letter and my enclosed resume. In the meantime, please let me know if you need additional information from me. Thank you in advance for your consideration.

Sincerely,

Carrie S. Yu
Carrie S. Yu

Encl.: resume

Final

Sample cover letter of Frank Douglas (weak or no connection).

Frank D. Douglas

1234 Lindell Blvd., Apt. W-504   (609) 123-4567
St. Louis, MO 63108   fddouglas@wustl.edu

January 25, 20XX

Mr. Thomas Winston
U.S. Environmental Protection Agency
Region III (3RC00)
1650 Arch Street
Philadelphia, PA 19103-2029

Dear Mr. Winston,

As a first-year student at Washington University School of Law ("Law School"), I am writing to express my interest in the Legal Internship ("Internship") at the Environmental Protection Agency ("EPA") office in Philadelphia. Past participants and fellow law students, Roseanne Brown and John Caruthers, recommended that I apply.

My lifelong interest in environmental issues, research skills, and ability to communicate would make me an effective EPA intern. My interest in the environment, particularly climate change, is one of the reasons I decided to attend law school. As an attorney, I want to use my passion and legal knowledge to impact policies that will benefit future generations. As an undergraduate, I studied the environmental consequences of globalization, philosophical problems of climate change, and rational choice theory behind international environmental agreements. While I have not had the opportunity as a first-year law student to take environmental law classes, I have dedicated my personal time to working with the Law School's Energy and Environmental Law Society as an elected board member. In that capacity, I have learned more about climate change and broadened the scope of my interest in environmental issues. I earned one of my highest grades this past semester in legal research, and am anxious to put that skill into practice in the environmental area. Prior to law school I taught English as a Second Language as part of a ministry program. As a teacher, I learned to communicate effectively with supervisors and students. My passion for the environment, research ability and communication skills would be an asset to the EPA.

I will be in the Philadelphia area in March and welcome the opportunity to meet with you or one of your colleagues then to learn more about the Internship and share my thoughts on why I would be an asset to the program. I will contact you in a few weeks to confirm that you received this letter and my enclosed resume and to see if there is a convenient time for us to meet in March. In the meantime, if you have any questions, please contact me. Thank you for your consideration.

Sincerely,

Frank D. Douglas
Frank D. Douglas

Encl.: Resume

Final

Sample cover letter of Sally Nathan (weak or no connection).

Sally Nathan
123 Lake Drive
Kirkwood, MO 63122
(314) 123-4567
snathan@wustl.edu

January 5, 20XX

Sara Cook, Esquire
Recruiting Chair
Smith Jones, LLP
800 Washington Avenue, Suite 2000
St. Louis, MO 63101

Dear Ms. Cook,

As a 1L student at Washington University Law School, I am reaching out to you as one of our alumni to get more information about your practice. Like you, I am from St. Louis and plan to practice law here. After working in Chicago and Dallas, it is nice to be back in St. Louis. In reviewing your firm's website, I noticed that Smith Jones has a large energy practice group. Given my experience in the oil and gas industry, I am interested in exploring energy law, and welcome the opportunity to speak with you or your colleagues about my background and the possibility of an internship for this coming summer.

I am confident that my work experience combined with my professional qualities would make me an asset to your firm this coming summer. During my legal internship at an entrepreneurial and patent law firm in Chicago, I worked closely with senior attorneys and their clients on a variety of litigation related matters, and was responsible for reviewing filings and assisting in litigation proceedings. As the account manager for a Dallas-based global contractor, I worked with multiple Fortune 500 energy companies. In that role, I gained extensive exposure to the oil and gas industry working face-to-face with clients regarding their insurance, quality, and regulatory information. I was also active in business development by organizing and leading prospect meetings while providing exceptional customer service to strengthen current client relationships. I continue to bolster my professional leadership and business development skills in law school as an elected representative of the Student Bar Association ("SBA"). My participation in the SBA has allowed me to work with my fellow students as well as law school administrators to insure that 1Ls' interests are recognized and addressed. An internship with Smith Jones would allow me to use my work experience, provide me the opportunity to learn from skilled attorneys, and hone my research, writing, and advocacy skills.

I would greatly appreciate the opportunity to meet with you or one of your colleagues to discuss my qualifications for a summer internship. I will follow up with a phone call within the next couple of weeks to confirm that you received this letter and my enclosed resume. Before then, please let me know if you need additional information from me. Thank you in advance for your consideration.

Sincerely,

Sally Nathan
Sally Nathan

Encl.: resume

Final

Sample cover letter of Stacy Stevens (weak or no connection).

Stacy A. Stevens
stacyastevens@wustl.edu
(504) 123-4567

January 25, 20XX

Rochelle Miller, Esquire
Carter Golden Legal Aid
123 N. Michigan Avenue
Chicago, IL 60642

Dear Ms. Miller:

I became interested in Carter Golden Legal Aid after Executive Director Mathew Bruner's presentation in St. Louis this fall. As a first-year law student at Washington University School of Law, I am excited to learn of an opportunity to engage in public service in Chicago. I am pursuing law school because I have a desire to provide justice for those who lack access to it and I believe that individuals can affect change one life at a time. I am drawn to Carter Golden because of its vision to empower people and their communities. Your CLAIM program and Criminal Records division are excellent examples of the multifaceted impact attorneys can have on men, women, children, and society as a whole. Please consider this letter and my enclosed resume as my application for an internship position this summer.

My passion for social justice, and my work experience and academic achievements in law school, will allow me to be a valuable and immediate contributor to your office as a legal advocate. My desire for social change and public service was first fueled by research and discourse for a class called Poverty, Justice & Capabilities. That course inspired my commitment to finding a way to engage hands-on with issues of the education gap, housing discrimination, miscarriages of justice, and wealth disparity. I was fortunate to work with Chicago's homeless population at Inspiration Café and youth at the Boys and Girls Club. As part of my work, I generated solutions for stretching non-profit resources to address multiple levels of clients' wellbeing. Throughout my time with Teach for America, I battled the interplay between education, class, family structure, and race as I implemented individualized plans for students and engaged their families in fighting for students' futures. As the Logistics Coordinator for a yearlong mission trip, I strengthened my leadership, communication, and time management skills. I coordinated with multiple parties, led large groups of diverse personalities, drove teams to complete time-sensitive projects, and balanced varied roles and responsibilities.

In addition to my passion for social justice, I understand the need for working with the system to effect change. In law school, I am integrating my real world experiences with legal concepts, analytical skills, and legal training. I was proud to score in the top fifteen percent in Legal Practice (legal writing) last semester. This past semester, I was also honored to be a Finalist in the Client Counseling Competition for 1Ls.

I welcome the opportunity to use my skills and growing legal knowledge to advance your mission of bringing justice and mercy to those with the greatest need. It would be my pleasure to interview for an internship with you and I would be happy to provide any further information you may require. I will contact you in a few weeks to confirm that you received this letter and my enclosed resume and to see if there is any other information you need from me to consider my application for an internship with Carter Golden.

Sincerely,

Stacy A. Stevens
Stacy A. Stevens

Encl.: resume

Appendix E

Action Verbs for Resumes and Cover Letters by Skill Category

Action Verbs for Resumes and Cover Letters by Skill Category

Note: bolded words used often in legal resumes and cover letters

Research and Writing Skills:

analyzed
assembled
assessed
authored
co-authored
collected
composed
conducted
conveyed
convinced
corresponded
counseled
critiqued
defined
documented
drafted
edited
evaluated
examined
explored
gathered
identified
interpreted
interviewed
investigated
organized
published
researched
reviewed
summarized
surveyed
tracked

Communication Skills:

addressed
advised
advocated
articulated
answered
clarified
collaborated
communicated
condensed
consulted
contacted
conveyed
corresponded
counseled
described
developed
directed
discussed
drafted
edited
educated
ensured
expedited
explained
facilitated
formulated
furthered
incorporated
informed
insured
interacted
interpreted

interviewed

judged

lobbied

mediated

moderated

motivated

negotiated

observed

outlined

participated

persuaded

presented

promoted

proposed

provided

published

publicized

reconciled

recruited

referred

reported

resolved

responded

reviewed

simplified

solicited

spoke

summarized

supported

synthesized

translated

volunteered

Management and Leadership Skills:

achieved

administered

advocated

aided

analyzed

appointed

approved

assigned

attained

authorized

chaired

completed

consolidated

contracted

converted

coordinated

delegated

developed

directed

eliminated

emphasized

enhanced

established

expanded

exceeded

fostered

generated

guided

handled

headed

hired

improved

increased

initiated

instituted

led

managed

mentored

merged

monitored

motivated

organized

originated

outperformed

oversaw

planned

presided

produced

recommended

recruited

reorganized

replaced

resolved

restored

reviewed

scheduled

spearheaded

streamlined

strengthened

supervised

surpassed

trained

Financial and Business Related Skills:

acquired

adjusted

allocated

analyzed

appraised

assessed

audited

balanced

calculated

computed

corrected

determined

developed

estimated

forecasted

managed

marketed

measured

planned

projected

reconciled

reduced

Teaching and Coaching Skills:

adapted

advised

clarified

coached

communicated

conducted

coordinated

critiqued

developed

encouraged

evaluated

explained

facilitated

focused

guided

individualized

informed

instructed

motivated

persuaded

secured

stimulated

taught

trained

transmitted

tutored

Epilogue

I thought you would find it interesting to know what the students whose resumes and cover letters were used as examples in this book did after their 1L year. They all had legal internships in the U.S., Africa, and Asia, and worked in non-profit, for-profit, and government legal organizations.

Specifically, the students had internships in the following organizations:

1. Global public interest legal organization in Africa;
2. National leadership fellowship in Illinois Legal Aid organization;
3. Medium-sized Midwestern law firm;
4. Large private national law firms;
5. California Appellate Project in San Francisco;
6. State public defender's office;
7. U.S. Attorney's Office for the Southern District of New York;
8. Neighborhood Legal Services in Washington, D.C.;
9. Bank of China; and
10. New Jersey Division of Law.

Index